Praise for
Fall of the Phantom Lord

"Todhunter . . . provides a useful primer not only on rock climbing but also on bouldering and alpine climbing, carefully delineating the different skills each sport demands. With his account of Osman's stunts, Todhunter mixes lengthy descriptions of his own daredevil exploits . . . [as] he tries to come to terms with why people do such things . . . It's enough to make you doubt, just a little, that hitting a baseball is the hardest thing to do in sports."—*The New York Times Book Review*

"A haunting read."—*Sports Illustrated*

"Classic participant-observer journalism—informed and heady—that brightly illuminates the strange, enthralling world of risk sports."
—*Kirkus Reviews*

"In this elegantly written book, Andrew Todhunter explores the pursuit of fear as the effort to find 'or make' one's character. The achievement is in the effort. Or, specifically, in the climb, and the story he writes is frightening and thrilling. Todhunter has produced a work of clear beauty and a true adventure of the soul."—**Roger Rosenblatt**

". . . at its pounding heart an engrossing psychological study of men and women who put their lives at risk as a way of deliberately facing and conquering fear. The author communicates that fear (often his own) with marrow-chilling honesty."—**Charles Champlin, Arts Editor** Emeritus, *Los Angeles Times*

"In this gripping, powerfully personal book, Andrew Todhunter makes the intricacies of rock and ice climbing—and diving on a rope from vast heights—into a study of the addictive raptures of risk, of technical knowledge pitted against death.—**Richard Meryman, author of** *Andrew Wyeth: A Secret Life*

climbing
and the face
of fear

andrew
todhunter

Anchor
Books

a division of
Random House, Inc.

new york

fall

of the

phantom

lord

ANCHOR BOOKS TRADE PAPERBACK EDITION

Copyright © 1998 by Andrew Todhunter

Portions of this work were originally published in
The Atlantic Monthly.

The Library of Congress has cataloged the Anchor
hardcover edition of this work as follows:
Todhunter, Andrew.
    Fall of the Phantom Lord: climbing and the face
of fear / by Andrew Todhunter.

        p.   cm.
    1. Mountaineering—United States.
2. Todhunter, Andrew.   3. Osman, Dan.
I. Title.
GV199.4.T63   1998
796.52'2'0973—dc21   98-15000
                                                        CIP

ISBN 0-385-48642-1

Book design by Maria Carella

www.anchorbooks.com

Printed in the United States of America

For Erin

Photo by Andrea Osman Brown

acknowledgments

Spanning a period of three years, the research and writing of this book required enormous tolerance and support from family, friends, subjects, and countless others who in a multitude of ways helped me through. Now, nearing publication, there is a growing sense of exhilaration, gratitude, and renewed curiosity, as if, having crossed a difficult continent, one comes at last to an unnamed sea.

My thanks must go first to Dan Osman, who while in my company was as generous and patient a subject and host as a writer could possibly deserve. I am likewise indebted to my other subjects, particularly those with whom I spent the greatest time, including Geoff Maliska, Nikki Warren, Coral Warren, and Jason Kuchnicki. Many thanks as well to Les Osman, Nanci Nelson, and Jay Smith.

Four years have passed since the death of Bobby Tarver. I did not have the pleasure of meeting him, but I offer my sincere condolences to his family and friends.

Many thanks to my agent, Candice Fuhrman, and to her assistants, Haden Blackman and Elsa Dixon, for their help in finding the book a home.

My profound thanks to my editor at Anchor Books, Roger Scholl. His patience, keen eye, and enthusiasm were instrumental in bringing the book to completion. Thanks also to Stephanie Rosenfeld for inspired editorial assistance, Martha Levin for bringing the book aboard, designer Maria Carella, art director Mario Pulice, Harold Grabau and the Copy Editing Department, freelance copy editor Bill Betts, publicist Jessica Stewart, and everyone else at Anchor Books for a magnificent job.

The book began as an article in the February 1996 issue of *The Atlantic Monthly*. My deepest thanks go to the magazine's managing editor Cullen Murphy, who gave me my start as a writer and has edited my work with great care and temperance for nearly a decade. Among the many at the magazine who deserve mention for work on this piece are William Whitworth, Barbara Wallraff, Martha Spaulding, Robin Gilmore-Barnes, and Katie Bacon.

I often turned to climbing experts, unrelated to the story, to help assure the objective accuracy of climbing material. Brian Mibach at Marin Outdoors and John Bouchard at Wild Things were invaluable in this regard. If mistakes survive to printing, I may have introduced them subsequent to their careful inspections; in any case, I am entirely to blame for any flaws or inconsistencies in the text. Thanks to Jim Bridwell and John Bachar for phone interviews.

Much of my historical and technical research had been done for me by writing climbers like Yvon Chouinard, whose *Climbing Ice* provided a host of valuable material, and Greg Child, who compiled *Climbing: The Complete Reference to Rock, Ice, and Indoor Climbing*. Always near at hand lay *Freedom of the Hills*, edited by Don Graydon. Much information was combed from the pages of *Rock & Ice* and *Climbing*.

For additional insights and material, I am grateful to Gay Roesch at the American Alpine Club library, as well as Eric Brand, Nick Clinch, Jed Williamson, Charlie Houston, Andy Selters, Mike Zanger, and the American Alpine Institute.

Having written much of the first draft under their roof, I am grateful to Ed Wall, Bill Sanderson, and the staff of the San Anselmo Coffee Roastery for their enduring hospitality.

Timothy Foote, Colin Foote, Gina Hahn, and Toby Morral helped enormously in the editing process. Thanks also to Bill Barich for his suggestions.

Many thanks to Wayne Greenwell, with whom I've shared a rope for many years, to Laura Elliot for her cherished counsel, and to Steve Mandel, whose optimism, entrepreneurial example, and advice were instrumental in my decision to forge a life as a freelance writer despite its notorious risks.

For his profound insight and guidance, I am deeply indebted to friend and adviser Phillip Moffitt.

Tobit Morral has been a dear friend, faithful critic, and loyal supporter for many years. His contributions to my life and work evade calculation.

I am very grateful to the members of my two families for their unquestioning support, especially Timothy Foote, Rosa Burke Perez and Jama Davis.

My very deepest gratitude, bound with awe, goes to my steadfast editor and wife Erin Davis Todhunter, and to our daughter Julia, who in eighteen months has given us joys beyond counting.

Andrew Todhunter
April 1998

part

one

At dawn on his thirty-second birthday, rock climber Dan Osman is poised to break the world record, his own, for a free fall from a standing structure. Using nothing more than the modified equipment of his trade, including single climbing ropes, a full body harness, and a reinforced anchor, he will jump an estimated 660 feet from a bridge in Northern California. The bridge soars some 700 feet above a wild river valley.

Osman's dark hair, long enough to cover his shoulder blades, is bound in a ponytail. Of mixed Japanese and European heritage, he is commonly mistaken as Native American. Weighing 155 pounds at five feet ten and a half, Osman is built like a gymnast.

During a safety meeting in the hours before departure for the bridge, Osman relegates tasks to the members of his support team—fellow climbers Geoff Maliska, twenty-three, Osman's unspoken disciple, and Anthony Meeks, twenty. Maliska is gregarious and irreverent. Meeks—whom the other climbers have known for less than a week—is reticent and self-conscious. Together, they review the details of rigging and safety protocol.

Upon arrival at the site they move out across the girders of the bridge, beneath the traffic, far above the valley floor. The sky is clear. A light wind moves through the girders. Osman rigs the elaborate anchor—a nest of nylon loops, or runners, climbing rope, and aluminum hardware—near the middle of the bridge. Leaving Meeks to tend the anchor in the capacity of downrigger, Osman continues with Maliska another 160 feet across the span.

The greatest danger in a fall of such a distance, Osman believes, is not the failure of the system, but entanglement within the rope. The force of impact achieved at terminal velocity, he suspects, could bisect or decapitate a body wound in the 10.5-millimeter cord. On this jump, to practice extricating himself from entanglement should it ever accidentally occur, Osman will intentionally wrap himself in the rope as he falls. He will then uncoil himself and assume a safe position, all within the seven seconds before impact. The attempt is unprecedented.

When he nears the launching point, the rope hanging slack beneath the bridge in a huge arc, Osman ties in, securing the rope to his harness. Originating at this lateral distance from the anchor, much of the fall's inertia will be diverted upon impact into a rocketing swing five hundred feet across the valley floor. As opposed to falling directly from the anchor position, this decreases the chance of entanglement and keeps initial impact forces—a striking whip when the rope runs out of slack—within reasonable limits.

Osman thoroughly checks his harness and knots three times, then examines his clothing for anything that might affect his fall. He looks down the rope and signals Meeks. Meeks checks the anchor, returns the signal—all is clear.

Osman begins to scale a girder, gaining the height necessary to break the record of his previous fall. The beating of his heart becomes unmanageable and he stops. He clings, closes his eyes, and fights for air. He tries to breathe deeply, to slow his heart, to dilute the load of adrenaline. Electric shocks fire like needles in the muscles of his hands, arms, and legs. Breathing deeply, Osman beats back his fear and continues up the girder. He stops twice, each time climbing farther before the panic mounts again and overwhelms him.

At last he reaches his launching point and stops. He closes his eyes and breathes, emptying his mind.

Several minutes later he opens his eyes and looks out across the valley. Traffic drums intermittently overhead. There are fishermen in the river far below. He watches the movement of their rods. Their faint voices rise to the bridge.

Osman closes his eyes again and visualizes the entire sequence of his fall, dilating the seven seconds into eleven or twelve. He will execute three cartwheels; in the middle of the third cartwheel he will twist his body and wrap himself one full turn in the rope. He will then unwrap—calmly, methodically, he will not thrash, he will not thrash—and extend his limbs, relaxing as he enters the point of impact. It is only when he completes the visualization that the risk of what he is about to attempt becomes clear. In the wake of this realization his fear leaps to the next plateau. Sweat runs from his pores and freezes. Goose bumps rise across his skin.

He glances down at Maliska and signs thumbs-up. Maliska is chilled by the horror in Osman's locked, Medusan gaze—he later claims that he has never seen Osman more visibly afraid—but he grins and returns the affirmative gesture. "Happy sailing," he calls.

Osman looks out across the valley. He steps through what he calls the moment of choice. He shifts his weight slightly over his feet. From fifteen, Osman counts down silently, breathing, saying only the ten and the five aloud. As he counts, Osman draws a breath. Four, three, two, one. As he exhales, he springs from the girder, into the open air. And then he falls.

.   .   .

As a boy, I spent many unwise hours climbing with friends on Hook Mountain, in Rockland County, New York. The Hook is a geological appendage of the Palisades, which rise like a curtain along the western bank of the Hudson River north of the George Washington Bridge. We climbed unroped, with little more in the way of equipment than canvas basketball shoes, cutoff shorts, and Yankee caps, and the degenerate rock came out in fistfuls like rotten teeth as we ascended.

We continued north on bikes along the river, past Haverstraw to the Bear Mountain Bridge. One afternoon we skidded down the steep embankment from the road to walk across the girders underneath the bridge. We trotted, then jogged back and forth across the grey-green rivet-studded beams, each one a foot, perhaps fifteen inches wide, leaning into gusts of wind to keep our balance, a hundred feet above the rocks along the river's eastern shore.

In the fifteen years that intervene I have dabbled broadly in outdoor sports. I have surfed Mundaka, caved on Crete, and scuba dived beneath the frozen surface of high Sierran lakes, and on charitable days I bless this breadth of training and experience. More commonly, I berate myself as a dilettante. Nowhere is this pattern more visible than in my relationship to climbing. I have traversed glaciers in the North Cascades, rock climbed in the Rockies and Shawangunks, bouldered in areas from Fontainebleau to Joshua Tree, but technically I remain of middling skill. Beside the likes of Osman I am not even a climber. In the cheerfully unminced words of Geoff Maliska, I am a flatlander.

Like legendary sea-kayaker Steve Sinclair—who paddled his specialized craft along the California coast in winter gales— Osman labors in my consciousness like a Titan, a figure of myth. Osman's myth is an old one: a man wrestles eternally upon a span, above a chasm. Locked in his arms is a dark angel, the Phantom Lord—not death itself, but fear of death. The man falls, finally, but the Phantom Lord falls with him. In the man's surrender lies the Phantom Lord's defeat.

I share Osman's fascination with fear and its management. As an adolescent, I courted danger with a near compulsion. Combined with an intractable resentment of authority, this often landed me in trouble. I was all but forced from one high school, expelled from another, and narrowly graduated from a third. I drove cars and later motorcycles at great speeds and with

extraordinary disregard, resulting in countless tickets, several accidents, and an arrest. At the time, I had little sense that my
behavior was unreasonable, that my troubles with authority had
more to do with me than with external forces. It took me a long
time to understand this, still longer to accept it.

On a shelf at the Crater Lake visitor center in Oregon, I
once discovered a book entitled *Bear Attacks*. The text recounted
in detail, with analysis, numerous attacks on humans by bears of
all kinds. I bought the book and read it in two sittings, in-
trigued most of all by the victims' varying responses to these
attacks. Some played dead, as commonly directed, and were left
alone. Others did so and were killed before the eyes of treed
companions. Still others fought back, with similarly mixed results. Not long ago, a Californian surfer was attacked by a Great
White and dragged several hundred yards across the surface.
The surfer fought the shark, clawing at its eyes and beating with
his fists, until it let him go. Blood clouding the water behind
him, the man swam back to shore. Surprised, probably, by the
surfer's spirited defense, the shark did not double back to finish
him off. The surfer required hundreds of stitches and a transfusion; given the extent of his injuries, his survival was miraculous.
Later, from his hospital bed, he said without irony that the
attack had been the single best experience of his life. A surprising comment, on the face of it, but I believe I know what he
meant.

My earliest memories of fear were of my father's temper. It
would let loose beneath us like a sun-warmed cornice, and there

was nothing we could do but ride it out. He didn't drink, but in the midst of his rages it was as if he had been struck by lightning. His anger was terrifying, but in its pure, elemental power it was awesome. It threatened to destroy, and yet, in some primitive way, it made me feel more alive. I hated him, for a while, when he quieted, and had no room for his apologies. But on some level, my father's anger bound us together. I think I suspected that his rages simply came in measure with his devotion. My father's moods were mixed terrain, but they were better, I believed, than indifference.

Later, I did not consciously take risks to reexperience my father's anger, or in obeisance of genetic imperatives, although these and other forces may well have been at work. I took risks, and to a lesser degree continue to do so, because it feels good to take risks. We may eat chocolate, scientists claim, in part because chocolate replicates the human chemical response to feeling loved. But we don't think about it that way; we eat chocolate because we like the way it tastes. Not everyone, even in the same family, likes adrenaline. My older brother, a hiker and onetime land surveyor with a shared appreciation of the outdoors, intensely dislikes the sensations that accompany physical fear. He takes great care, he says, to avoid them, and there are serious climbers who feel the same way.

Despite its attendant dangers, rock climbing—Osman's specialty—is poorly designed for the adrenaline addict. It is hard work, for one thing, and often meditative. Excess adrenaline undermines any climber's necessary focus. But underneath it all, the undeniable factor of risk elevates the sport into a discipline of deadly seriousness. You can be killed climbing, by a single misstep, a single mistied knot.

While rock climbing at reasonable altitudes, protected by the rope, the risks are not outlandish. At this writing, the number of regular climbers in the United States (those who own their own equipment and climb at least ten weekends a year) has been estimated in excess of 250,000 souls, a number that has doubled four times since 1980. Several hundred thousand more Americans have tried some kind of climbing at least once. Some thirty, on average, die every year. Of these, less than half involve rock climbers on protected routes. But the penalties for inattention are merciless.

All of these factors are on some level at play when I arrive in South Lake Tahoe in the late winter of 1995. I am eager to meet Osman, to climb with him, to watch him climb and fall. I hope to achieve some understanding of what drives him to the extremes he occupies. To that end, I plan to take an introductory fall on his rope.

And yet my life is changing. I am recently married, with a family, we hope, on the horizon. My notions of what I owe, and to whom, are shifting, and my relationship to climbing and to risk is changing with it. In Osman's company, I may come to find the line I will not cross.

. . .

Shortly before three in the afternoon on the third of February 1995, a rope lies loosely gathered at the base of a decomposing granite outcropping known as the Pie Shop. Osman, Meeks, and I have come to spend a half day climbing at the site. Two hundred feet high, girdled with a sloping, snow-clad boulder field, the outcropping rises from the relative flats southwest of Lake Tahoe. From its peak, a small airport is visible to the south. The site was named for a popular coffeehouse and pie shop— long since vanished—frequented by climbers at the nearest intersection of Route 50 and Sawmill Road.

Unwinding from its center, its end affixed to Osman's harness, the rope follows the ravine between two stones, rises through the shivering branches of a manzanita bush, and moves vertically across the granite face. Diamondbacked in fluorescent orange, yellow, and green, the rope is slightly less than nine millimeters in diameter. The accumulated friction of its passage produces an amplified hiss in the windless silence which ebbs and swells in rhythm with the climber above. Here on the exposed southern flank of the outcropping, in direct sun, the late winter air is warm.

Despite the rope attached to his harness, Osman is free-soloing the 165-foot climb. That is to say, he is climbing unprotected by the rope, and any fall will send him to the earth. He is merely "tailing" the rope to the top of the outcropping for use as protection in a later, more difficult climb. The route he follows is called *Earn Your Wings*.

Osman began climbing at age twelve, with the encouragement of his mother, Sharon Louise Burks, a horse trainer and two-time world champion barrel racer (a rodeo event involving agile horses, standing barrels, and figure eights). Despite his evident talent, he describes himself as a slow developer; it took him eight years to climb 5.12, a technical rating in rock climbing still generally considered to represent the start of expert difficulty. He now ranks among the country's finest rock climbers.

Climbers speak of elegance—elegance of climbing style, of route. It is undeniable that climbing without rope is more elegant than climbing roped, as climbing roped but mechanically unaided is more elegant than gadgeting skyward with ascenders and short nylon rope ladders, called étriers. The catch of free-soloing, and its appeal, is the simplicity of the equation it demands: one cannot fall. Like kendo practitioners who lay aside their wooden swords to duel with live blades, the climber—in abandoning the rope on routes where falling is synonymous with extinction—becomes a kind of mystic.

In preparation for a difficult solo Osman will climb the route several times on rope, repeating the crux, or most difficult move of the route, until certain he can execute the climb without error. "Then I start breathing," he explains, "to get the *ki* down into my *hara.*"

Loosely translated from the Japanese as "vital energy," *ki* is not a cultural abstraction, but a tangible phenomenon, as significant to the martial artist as harmony is to the musician. The *hara* (literally "belly"), an area in the abdomen below the navel, is held to be the center and source of physical energy. It serves as a reservoir of sorts in which *ki,* largely through breath control, may be pooled and from which it may be directed.

"I visualize a screen," Osman says, "a steel filter that I lower with my breaths to keep the positive energy. I let the fear and negative energy escape." When he is centered—a process that takes from five to twenty minutes—he is ready to climb. "I feel the air pressure," he says. "The *ki* is very concentrated, very strong. I feel the gravity more. When I step onto the rock, my senses immediately sharpen. The taste in my mouth becomes vivid."

In the 1890s Osman's paternal great-grandfather, a descendant of samurai families in the Takeuchi clan, emigrated to Hawaii from the mountainous Iwakuni region of Japan. Takeuchi was shot and killed in 1910 on a sugar plantation in the act of disarming a fellow laborer bent on assassinating their foreman. Born in Corona, California, Osman was trained as a boy in the samurai ethic of bushido by his father, Les Osman, a twenty-one-year-veteran police officer. At his father's encouragement, the young Osman studied aikido and later kung fu. The elder Osman, initially critical of his son's vocation, is now outspokenly supportive. "In climbing he found something where he could test himself against himself. He met the tiger and he didn't run. He walked away."

Although the general meaning of this comment is clear, I am confused by its concluding sentence. If the tiger is Osman's fear, then he is certainly not running from it. And yet, by pushing the grade as a climber, and by jumping from bridges, I do not see how he has walked away, or even merely stood his ground. Someday, perhaps, he may let his terrors come to him. But now, by my measure, he aggressively pursues the tiger of his father's metaphor. The younger Osman does not turn his back to fear. He tracks it, baits it, and withstands its rush.

・
・
・
・
・
・
・

Despite the ease of *Earn Your Wings* for a climber of his ability, Osman appears to spare nothing. His pace is unhurried. The expression on his face is a void. Even on large, so-called positive holds, the placement of his hands and feet—the latter tightly shod in pale blue, red-laced rock shoes soled in sticky black rubber—is unerringly precise. Without interrupting the liquid flow of his movement he seems to consider each hold as if preparing to catch the raised head of an asp. When he makes his placement, it is final. There is no shuffle, no grope. For all his fluidity, there is an awesome mechanical beat to his progress. Bang. Bang. Bang. Bang. He seems to climb within a field generated by the concentration of his will.

In North America, climbs are rated according to the Yosemite Decimal System, devised by the Sierra Club Mountaineers in the 1930s. From Class 1, walking, and Class 2, scrambling, the rating mounts to difficult and exposed "free-climbing" at Class 5, and concludes with "aid-climbing" at Class 6.

Often confused by the layman with free-soloing, free-climbing is to climb a route using nothing but natural holds— cracks, flakes, pockets, and other imperfections of the rock— without the aid of mechanical devices in resting or ascent. In free-climbing, such devices may be used only as protection, set in place along the route to catch an accidental fall. So-called aid is employed on routes where natural hand- and footholds are nonexistent or so negligible that mechanical assistance is required to ascend. Essentially, the aid climber rests and climbs with his or her weight placed directly on the mechanical anchors. Typically, this requires the use of étriers. A pair of climbers could thus leapfrog up a steeply overhanging face of perfect marble, provided they were willing to drill bolts. Long, multiday climbs, particularly those found on big walls like Yosemite Valley's El Capitan, often mix free- and aid-climbing; a superior climber may be able to "free" what a less experienced climber must "aid." Landmarks in climbing occur when classic routes—long believed to require aid—finally "go free," or surrender entirely to a free ascent.

Class 5 is subdivided through the addition of an unorthodox decimal system, further nuanced by a plus or minus (5.8+) or even more precisely (on climbs of 5.10 and above) with a letter, *a* through *d.* The distinction between a 5.12d and a 5.13a is often subtle enough to be a matter of debate. The difference of a full decimal point, however, is substantial; until recently, a dedicated climber could expect to spend months or even years advancing from 5.10 to 5.11, from 5.11 to 5.12. With the likes of Katie Brown and Chris Sharma (children of thirteen at the time of my first visit with Osman), climbing 5.12 within months of taking up the sport, and dominating the adult competitive climbing circuit a year later, the rules have begun to change. Many credit their astonishing success to the intense training afforded by gym climbing, continuing refinements in equipment and technique, and perhaps most important, a mental edge possessed by these young climbers: they are not intimidated by numerical ratings; they are not afraid to try and fail.

When the Yosemite Decimal System was implemented, the world's best climbers could not imagine a route as difficult as 5.7. At the time, then, there was no imaginable conflict, mathematically, with a decimal system in which the next whole number—6—was unavailable, taken as it was to define a wholly different style of climbing. We would never need the ratings 5.8 or 5.9, climbers argued—routes that technically demanding were not humanly possible—so there was no need to worry about decimally rear-ending Class 6. By 1952, when the first, miraculous 5.9 was climbed *(Open Book* at Tahquitz Rock, in Southern California), by Royal Robbins and Don Wilson, the decimal ceiling loomed suddenly overhead. The climbing community scrambled for a solution. Some—the more mathematically compulsive among them—suggested usurping Class 6 for the advancement of free-climbing and assigning a different value to aid-climbing. Certain aid climbers, unsurprisingly, protested. Someone else suggested breaking 5.9 down into subdecimals: 5.91, 5.92, 5.93. But no one liked the sound of climbing 5.9999—the all-but-certain future of that solution—so the idea was dropped. Then someone came up with a brilliant stroke of illogic, of mathematical impossibility. "How about five-ten?" he proposed in a meek voice. "Followed, if need be, by five-eleven." The mathematicians howled. "Five-ten? That's *six!* Or else it's five-one-oh, in which case we're going backward." But 5.10 stuck. And the beauty of it lies in the fact that it can go on forever, eternally ignorant of mathematical law. Five-twenty. Five-thirty. Five ninety-nine. Uh-oh.

Earn Your Wings is a 5.9. Arguably the most difficult free climb in the world at writing—infamous for its dynamic, one-finger moves—is *Action Directe*, 5.14d, in Germany, established, or "placed," by the late Wolfgang Güllich. Believed by many to be the greatest free-climber in the history of rock climbing, Güllich was killed in an auto accident in 1992 at the age of thirty-one.

In order to complete the route, Güllich gradually trained the tendons of his index and middle fingers until he could perform repetitive one-finger, one-armed pull-ups without injury. This alone would have been adequate if the route demanded nothing but static one-finger moves. A static move—as opposed to a dynamic, or lunging, move—is one in which the climber's weight is gradually shifted from one position to the next. Dynamic moves, or "dynos," are required when the next available hold lies beyond the climber's natural reach. The climber jumps through the air, in effect, to the next hold. Commonly, the target of a dyno is generous—a large pocket or horn that is easy to grasp, possibly with both hands. To throw a dyno and land on a single-finger pocket—a feat previously unheard-of—Güllich perfected a technique called dead-pointing. He trained himself to leap with precisely enough force to arrive within reach of the hold in the dead point of his arc. He learned to place his finger during that weightless instant, at the apex of his jump, when he was neither rising nor falling. With his finger in position, he cushioned the subsequent landing by extending his bent arm like an expanding spring, and diverting as much weight as possible to his feet, connected through friction to the rock below.

Completing *Earn Your Wings*, Osman proceeds to solo a

short piece of his own design: *Funky Cold Medina,* 5.10a, a corner overhanging 160 feet of air.

A difficult route can take months for a climber to place. The completed route is christened and rated by its author. "It's an historic moment," says Osman. "A first ascent can never be repeated." Subsequent climbers will confirm or challenge the rating—climbs are often downrated as climbers work out easier sequences over time—and soon the route will appear, immortalized, in local climbing guides.

Osman takes immense care in the creation of his routes, his greatest satisfaction praise from other climbers for the spare beauty of his lines. "A climb is not an opponent," he says. He regards each climb as a monument, not only to its creator but to the climbers of generations past who attempted the route unsuccessfully—with equal boldness but inferior technology—as well as to those who follow and attempt the route.

Osman takes many of the names for his routes from the titles of heavy-metal bands or songs, including *Chemikill, Anesthesia, Malice in Chains, Overkill,* and *Mandatory Suicide.* Like Osman's taste for heavy-metal music itself, these names are somehow surprising, out of sorts with their courteous and soft-spoken adopter. Osman's behavior is sharply governed, on the one hand, by the values of tradition, respect, and self-restraint. On the other, he reveals a profound rebelliousness and disregard for commonly accepted limitations. As a climber, this duality has taken him far. As a citizen—as a motorist, in particular—it has caused him grief. If Osman is a postmodern samurai, he is certainly a *ronin*, or "wave-tossed warrior," an outlaw of sorts, a knight without a lord.

From *Funky Cold Medina* Osman moves left across the shoulder of the outcropping, to another of his creations, *Buttons of Gold*, 5.9+, named for the tawny nipples of rock that serve as holds. He then moves through the boulders that crown the broad-backed monolith, executes short, powerful sequences on overhangs, leaps from stone to stone.

Osman moves east across the flattened peak of the outcropping, the coiled rope over his shoulder. He steps lightly in his rock shoes over beards of crusted snow, drops through a notch, and emerges beneath and to the side of a swollen bulge of granite that droops over the outcropping's southern face like the cap of an enormous mushroom. A horizontal crack, centimeters to inches in width, runs laterally forty feet along the joint between the bulge and the face, then curves obliquely to disappear from view. From this crack a climber who fell unchecked would travel 280 feet to the ground, glancing once from a sloping ledge midway. The route is *Blood in My Chalk Bag*, 5.11c/d.

Osman has free-soloed the route on three occasions. Today he believes he lacks the necessary mental edge, and will climb it roped. I ask him why he feels unprepared. "Too much coffee," he explains. "I could feel some shake on *Earn Your Wings*. And I'm a little tired, distracted. It's very subtle; I'd never notice it on the ground. But I know I don't have the focus to solo it." He sets the anchor, ties in, and dipping his fingers into a pouch at his waist, whitens both sides of his hands with chalk. Powdered gymnastic chalk marginally protects the hands and keeps them dry of sweat, improving their grip.

Meeks squats on a ledge near the beginning of the route; he will serve as Osman's belayer. Anchored through his harness to a boulder, Meeks feeds the rope through a belaying device which will help him brace a potential fall.

Osman moves out across the section of face between the belay ledge and the overhang. He pulls himself into a hemispherical notch in the rock, rests on his heels, and rechalks his hands. He grimaces faintly, nagged by three recently broken ribs (snowboard, tree), and stretches his torso. He releases a breath, then drops out of the notch and begins the climb, moving horizontally along the crack.

The footholds on the nearly vertical face below the crack are thin. Most of Osman's weight, in a technique known as smearing, is supported by the friction of his sticky rubber soles against the texture of the granite. He carefully jams his left hand deep into the crack. With his right he unclips a spring-loaded camming device—idiomatically known as a cam—from a loop on his harness. Holding the device like a depressed syringe, he inserts the retracted head into a section of the crack best suited to its width. When he releases the trigger, the opposing cams, or curved wedges, expand and seize the rock with dull metal teeth. He tests the piece with a tug, clips his rope into the carabiner that dangles from the unit by a nylon loop, and continues. Ubiquitous in climbing, the carabiner is an oblong ring of aluminum alloy about the length of an avocado and equipped with a spring-loaded gate. A semantic cousin of the Carabiniere, Italy's elite paramilitary police force, the carabiner was originally invented to clip carbine rifles to bandoleers and may still serve that function. The lightest climbing carabiner's minimum breaking strength in the direction of its long axis is 2,000 kilograms, or about 4,400 pounds.

While still well below the limit of Osman's ability, *Blood in My Chalk Bag* is rigorous. In contrast to his style on *Earn Your Wings,* Osman's execution here is simian, dynamic, a display of tenacity and brute strength. Some of his positions appear awkward, out of balance, but he is climbing as the route demands. With his right hand and right foot jammed into the crack, Osman pauses briefly, hangs to rest, slackens his opposing limbs. Soon he vanishes around the bulge and finishes the climb.

He reappears minutes later, dropping through the notch to rejoin us on the belay ledge. Meeks decides to follow, cleaning the route of its protection as he goes. Osman will belay. Meeks sets off along the route but is soon in trouble. Although the climber is skilled on faces, his crack technique is no match for the route. His progress is painstaking. Osman coaches, move by move. The light fails in the snow-dusted valley below. The temperature drops. A cam resists extraction. Meeks wrestles with the recalcitrant piece, swears at it, finally falls. Osman braces and holds Meeks in place. Meeks hangs on the protection and rests. The darkness deepens. Temporarily placing another device beside it to relieve his weight, Meeks finally gets the cam out and continues. He finishes the climb and appears on the crest of the bulge, stands silhouetted in the dying sky.

Osman is not his teacher, but the role is unavoidable given

the discrepancy in age and skill. Coiling the rope, he praises Meeks's effort but gently reprimands him for not being entirely honest with himself or with Osman, given the route, his ability, the time and conditions. Meeks nods, abashed. In the silence that follows, he holds out his hands as if examining a manicure. He looks thoughtfully at the blood-spotted chalk on his knuckles and smiles with pride.

We rappel through the darkness and by the light of Osman's headlamp pack our gear and file between boulders through the snow to his truck, parked on the shoulder of Sawmill Road. The vehicle is a 1984 tan Toyota with more than 213,000 miles on the engine. The rear bumper is graced with the images of Beavis and Butt-head, dressed, respectively, in Metallica and AC/DC T-shirts. Not far from their leering, pimpled faces is a skull—a symbol of the Grateful Dead—worn through to the chrome. A Sawsall, a toolbox, a pair of ski poles, and a battered tape deck lie in the truck's covered bed. We throw our packs into the truck with crunching thuds and wedge ourselves into the small cab. A circular pin is affixed to the passenger's sun visor; it bears a photograph of Osman's daughter, Emma, at her kindergarten graduation ceremony, dressed in a sky-blue cap and gown. Emma is now eight, and lives with her mother, Katherine Noyes, in nearby Gardnerville, Nevada. Osman says that his relationship with Noyes failed, in large part, because of his devotion to climbing. Osman makes a U-turn and hurtles in the direction of South Lake Tahoe. He thumbs a cassette of heavy metal into the tape deck. The band is White Zombie. "When

I'm in the sky I'm too far away," wails the vocalist, all but indecipherable above the instrumental chaos.

Osman lives alone in a warm, sepulchral studio two hundred yards from the shore of Lake Tahoe. The bed, couch, chair, and table in the main room abut like puzzle pieces. Along one wall stands a workbench layered with climbing hardware: camming devices, chocks, carabiners, ice axes, snowshoes, crampons, a red helmet. Three books—*Joshua Tree: A Climbing Guide, Boulder Climbs South,* and *Fox in Socks,* by Dr. Seuss—lean against a milk crate nested with slings and spare harnesses. A coiled rope lies yoked over a vise. Propped against an electric guitar amplifier is a red and yellow backpack, a prototype of Osman's design for the North Face, perhaps the world's best-known manufacturer of expedition clothing and equipment. Two snowboards lean in the corner by the door. There is a small television, a VCR, and a collection of rock climbing videos. Seven or eight books stand on a bedside table, each of them concerned with Japanese history and the samurai, including an epic novel on the life of Miyamoto Musashi, Clavell's *Shōgun,* and *The Samurai Sword—a Handbook.*

From beneath his bed, Osman reverently withdraws a Japanese long sword, or *katana,* its curved scabbard sheathed in blackened sharkskin. The sword's hilt is veneered with the dimpled ivory hide of a stingray and bound in a lattice of burnt-orange silk. The wave-tempered blade is nicked and smudged in places by irreparable corrosion.

Returning from the Pacific as a war trophy with an American serviceman, the sword came into the hands of Les Osman at the cost of a bartered shotgun. Experts have since confirmed the weapon's age in excess of four hundred years. Reserving it for the occasion, the elder Osman presented the *katana* to his son in an informal ceremony on Thanksgiving of 1994. Believing himself undeserving, the younger Osman unsuccessfully attempted to decline.

"He had earned the right to have possession of the sword," Les Osman recalls. "Doing the work that I do, I have faced death many, many, many times. When it's over, you celebrate the fact that you're alive, you celebrate the fact that you have a family, you celebrate the fact that you can breathe. Everything, for a few instants, seems sweeter, brighter, louder. And I think this young man has reached a point where his awareness of life and living is far beyond what I could ever achieve."

Photographs of Osman's daughter, Emma, are visible from every angle in the apartment. On the walls are posters, a balance of heavy-metal bands—notably Metallica—and climbers on varying terrain. Twice appearing is Lynn Hill, a groundbreaking climber now working at the top of her form. Osman cites Hill, together with Jay Smith, Wolfgang Güllich, and legendary soloist John Bachar (pronounced *Backer*) as climbing exemplars.

Like many climbers, Osman is also a carpenter; as such he has earned a reputation for perfectionism. Nevertheless, he has been making a gradual shift into climbing professionally over recent years, weaning himself financially from fifty to ten hours a week in construction. To do so, he has cut back dramatically on his lifestyle; in five years he has pared his monthly expenses from

$1,200 to $700. "I tell people I'm getting out of construction," Osman says. "I don't like buying new tools because it means I'm still a carpenter; that I still can't support myself through climbing alone." This attitude may rankle among other, less fortunate climbers, striking them as precious in a field closer to the arts, in respect to income, than professional sports. "Real Musicians Have Day Jobs" I have spied on the bumpers of three pickup trucks—their beds choked with lumber—in the last six months. Only a fraction of serious climbers are in a position to earn their living climbing. Even at the top, there is simply not much to be had: free shoes, rope, and other equipment, a modest stipend of cash from the odd sponsor, the occasional photo incentive. Aggressive alpine guiding can provide a decent living, but no one—yet—is getting rich climbing.

For Osman, professional climbing began with a 1990 trip to the New River Gorge in West Virginia. After one ascent roped, repeating the first crux a dozen times to impress its sequence solidly into his memory, he free-soloed the 120-foot *Gun Club*, 5.12c. It was an astonishing feat—Jay Smith's still photographs of Osman at the second crux, 90 feet above the deck, are staggering—and established Osman as one of the country's preeminent free-soloists. Smith sold a photograph of the climb to a rock-climbing-shoe manufacturer. The resulting advertisement secured Osman his first contract: five pairs of shoes every year plus a photo incentive—he would receive a small fee for any photograph of him in their shoes appearing in the media. Other contracts followed: an unspecified quantity of free equipment from one company, $125-a-month salary together with free clothing from another, $500 per year plus a photo incentive from a third.

Sporadically, Osman teaches and guides climbers in the Tahoe area—on a good day, he can take home from $300 to $750. As an instructor, Osman has noticed that women usually do better than men as beginning climbers because, lacking upper-body strength, they focus on footwork. As much as 75 percent of a skilled climber's weight is on the feet, Osman estimates, even on overhanging terrain. More recently, his still or moving image—climbing or jumping—has appeared in several nonclimbing venues, including advertisements for sport utility vehicles, imported beer, aftershave, and a prominent national bank. All told, and just barely, Osman is now capable of paying his base expenses with climbing and stunt-related income alone.

The following morning Osman and company appear out of the mist at Cave Rock. The Cave, as it is known, is an ominous and nobly situated vault—like half of a basilica's dome—hewn by erosion from the andesite cliff far above the fog-swept eastern shoreline of Lake Tahoe. Despite the single lane of highway that passes not far below its base, it is the kind of cave, were it to be found in the Aegean, in which Olympian divinities were rumored to be born. The native Washo Indians—who sold the land around Lake Tahoe to white settlers for one cent per acre—have long considered the cave sacred.

Quickdraws—pairs of carabiners connected by short lengths of colorful nylon webbing—dangle from the cave's roof. The cave floor, once littered with condom wrappers, disposable diapers, and shards of green and amber glass left by adolescent revelers, is now a lithic garden. With help, Osman devoted more than three hundred hours to the construction of belay benches, gravel pathways, and austerely decorative stone formations. The result has been met with some criticism, notably from local climbers who resent the increase in climbing traffic in the wake of Osman's improvements. "They say they wish the cave was the same old dirty place it used to be," Osman relates, with some bitterness. "I've often considered tearing the whole thing out." One opponent, an erstwhile friend and climbing partner of Osman's, took a sledgehammer to the rock garden, then bashed handholds from one of Osman's routes, a 5.12 bouldering traverse near the floor of the cave. "He had always been infuriated," Osman says, "that he couldn't do the traverse."

A subclass of rock climbing with its own rating system, "bouldering" is climbing so close to the ground that no protective rope is required. Some of the world's most challenging bouldering routes, often woven from the pocketed roofs of caves, are so near the earth that a climber at the crux could reach down with one hand and touch the soil. From the tops of higher bouldering routes, a bad landing could break a leg, or worse. To help prevent injury, climbers on the ground will commonly "spot" their partners while they boulder, holding out their hands to help soften or arrest a potential fall. Before the invention of portable, brightly colored bouldering pads, old mattresses, moldering from exposure, were commonly found at popular bouldering areas. On giant rocks, in caves, or at the bases of larger faces, bouldering routes tend toward the technically extreme. Often steeply overhanging, such routes demand both power and precision. In addition to short vertical routes, traverses are extremely common.

Bouldering is an excellent way for a climber to rapidly gain strength and technique. In an hour and a half in a fertile bouldering area, a climber can pull more holds than in a long day of free-climbing. Bouldering, in short, provided many of the benefits of indoor climbing long before the appearance of climbing gyms. Among the world's many fine bouldering areas are those found in Fontainebleau, France, in Hueco Tanks, Texas, and at California's Joshua Tree National Monument.

· · ·

Osman steps from the gravel floor onto the wall of the cave. With the delicacy of a watchmaker and the strength of a longshoreman, he climbs up and out across the increasingly inverted roof. Maliska—his shoulder-length blond hair beneath an MTV cap, a pinch of chewing tobacco behind his lower lip—belays from the ground. The route Osman follows is his own: *Phantom Lord*, 5.13c.

"When I put up *Psycho Monkey* in 1989," explains Osman, "I had never climbed a 5.13. It took me nine months. It's rated 13b. At the time, I thought it was the hardest line at the cave. But when I finished it, I looked to the right and saw the line of *Phantom Lord*, which was harder. When I finished that, I looked to the right again and saw the 5.14 I'm working on now. One day, while I was working on that, I saw the line of *Slayer*. At the time, I thought it was going to be harder than all of them. I yelled to my belayer to lower me, and ran over to start working on it."

When Osman finished *Slayer*—a year-long project—in 1992, he rated it 5.14a. Soon after, however, climbers Doug Englekirk and Tom Herbert discovered easier sequences and downrated the route to 5.13d and .13c/d, respectively. Others have since concurred with Osman's original estimation—Wolfgang Güllich also praised the route as the most elegant he'd ever climbed—but *Slayer* stands on the books, more conservatively, at .13d. While frustrated, Osman nevertheless prefers a downgrade to suspicions of exaggerated difficulty. The 5.14 rating of his route in progress, Osman believes, will not be challenged.

To Osman's left on *Phantom Lord*, a Yugoslavian dental assistant climbs *Port of Entry*, 5.12a. She is belayed by her companion, a local carpenter. The sun appears, warming the interior of the cave. Maliska's dog, Kayla, a chow-retriever mix, lounges on the stones. Her left foreleg is wrapped in a cast; she recently leapt into the path of Maliska's snowboard. To the right, Meeks boulders on the start of *Asylum*, 5.12a.

Peter Millar, forty, a Stanford-trained chemist and design engineer, and Roger Rogalski, thirty-nine, an orthopedic surgeon, rest between climbs. While they watch Osman's progress, their bare arms crossed, the two men discuss amino acid strings and ordering principles in low tones. Minutes before, Rogalski—who hadn't climbed in several months as the result of an injury—casually ascended *Asylum*. With slightly more effort,

Millar just "sent," or successfully climbed, *Fire in the Hole,* 5.12b.

Aside from a couple of short bouldering problems to the right of the cave's mouth, there isn't a route within my ability at the cave.

Arriving at the end of the seventy-foot overhang, Osman rounds the lip of the cave and continues climbing on the cliff-side's natural contour. In three moves he reaches the anchor: a steel ring, or hanger, bolted to the rock. He has finished the route and for a moment rests. Then he prepares his fall.

Balanced on the face, he calls for slack. Maliska feeds the rope while Osman lowers it in a long loop between his harness and the anchor. The length of slack will be the distance of Osman's free fall: sixty-five feet. Maliska locks off the rope in his belaying device. Thus secured, he will serve as Osman's counterweight through the fulcrum of the anchor overhead. Upon Osman's impact on the rope, Maliska will spring skyward in the direction of the pull. The force of the fall will pluck him more than ten feet into the air. A less flexible belay would rob Osman of the necessary give and catapult him in and up against the cavern's jagged roof at a speed approaching sixty miles per hour. This potentially fatal error has already been made, by another belayer who leaned back instinctively to brace a similar but accidental fall. The resulting impact broke both of Osman's ankles.

Osman calls to Maliska. Maliska crouches slightly in position—poised to spring—and returns the call: all clear. Osman careens out away from the cliff and plummets earthward, limbs flung wide. He completes two cartwheels, swings gracefully into the lower recesses of the cave, and swoops silently back into space. Maliska hangs in his harness, legs braced against the wall, twelve feet above the gravel floor. Osman calls this jump the Phantom Leap.

To climb at the edge of your ability is to fall, and the equipment is designed to keep those falls from causing injury or death. But the equipment, on occasion, fails, and the climber fails more often than that. On rope or off, it is the fear of an unchecked fall—a bone-snapping, skull-crushing fall—that nags most climbers, holds them back, thwarts their inspiration.

In 1989, while ferreting from virgin overhanging rock the line of *Phantom Lord,* lunging for uncertain holds, Osman took fall after fall. He was belayed, protected by the rope, but like any climber with imagination, a part of him feared every fall for the worst. He realized then that it was not in climbing, but in falling, that he would embrace his fear—bathe in it, as he says— and move beyond it. He began to fall on purpose, from greater and greater heights. Osman's comfort and performance on the rock have improved accordingly.

In the process of perfecting such a fall, Osman has done more than simply grapple with his fears. By greatly exaggerating the conditions of normal climbing falls, he has in five years gathered enough data to potentially revolutionize the technology and application of climbing protection. He is currently experimenting with modified equipment, including protection and belaying devices, and is developing techniques—including body positioning before and during impact on the rope—to greatly improve the safety of long climbing falls.

"No one has ever taken these kind of impact loads on climbing equipment," says Osman. "The rope and equipment manufacturers test the gear with dummies, but dummies can't tell you what it feels like to fall on the equipment."

Standard sport climbing harnesses with narrow, unpadded belts are dangerous, Osman claims, for any but the shortest falls. "Climbers should be aware of what they're doing to their bodies with these harnesses on long whippers," he says, referring to long "leader falls," or falls taken by a lead climber. Depending on the body's position upon impact at rope's end, Osman claims that such insubstantial harnesses, favored for their light weight, can break ribs or damage kidneys.

Osman would like to see an industry standardization of rope stretch, together with logbooks provided by manufacturers with each rope. In such a log, the rope's owner could record the nature and distance of every leader fall taken. At the end of the rope's life, commonly from one to three years, the owner would return the rope and logbook to the manufacturer for analysis, and a modest rebate on their next rope.

Osman studies divers, parachutists, and acrobatic ski jumpers to learn more about manipulating his position in the air. Correct body position, he has learned, is critical to minimize the chance of injury on a long roped fall. "If you're going to take a huge whipper," says Osman, "I suggest taking it headfirst." Upon impact at the end of the rope, whichever end of the body is higher during the fall will rotate violently around the fulcrum of the harness and extend like a snapped towel, absorbing the force of the fall. Better your legs, Osman reasons, than your skull—with or without a helmet.

Properly applied, Osman's work will certainly prevent injuries and may well save lives on the rock. But there are costs. In May 1994 Bobby Tarver, a twenty-five-year-old bungee jumper in Osman's circle of close friends, was killed replicating one of Osman's falls. Unable to accompany Tarver to the site, Osman first attempted to forestall him, then precisely described and diagrammed each step in the fall's preparation. Tarver was impatient. "You could see it in his eyes," says Osman. "He was looking at the paper but he wasn't listening." With a handful of companions, Tarver proceeded to a bridge that spans a Utah canyon. In preparation for a long jump, he failed to stretch the rope—as Osman had explicitly directed—with a series of shorter falls. When he jumped, the rope stretched too far, and Tarver struck the sloping canyon wall 250 feet below. He swung into the middle of the canyon and dangled in the air until his friends could cut him down. He briefly regained consciousness and died three hours later.

Osman has returned to that bridge on numerous occasions since the accident, three times to jump. Twice he retreated from the edge. He finally descended into the canyon, spoke with Tarver, as he puts it, and remounted the bridge. Choosing to ignore technical refinements made since the tragedy, Osman jumped precisely—and successfully—according to the plan he diagrammed for Tarver on that morning in May.

Near dusk at Cave Rock, as the climbers break down their gear
on the gravel floor, a car slows and stops across the road. Its
driver, a climber, yells to Osman that he has left his truck's
lights on. This oversight surprises me, out of keeping as it is
with Osman's meticulous air. We hike along the road in our
packs, into the gathering darkness, and jump-start the truck
with a push.

Minutes later five of us tramp into a Chinese restaurant in
South Lake Tahoe. Hands and faces soiled, in sweaty, ragged
clothes and untied hiking boots, we are undeniably a motley
band. The proprietors greet us with smiles of polite dismay as we
shamble across the dining room to a corner booth. The service is
excruciatingly slow, and Maliska finally complains. Neighboring
diners eye our party warily. Meeks ducks under the table to go to
the rest room and returns. Trays finally arrive, laden with plates.
We eat voraciously for a time in silence. Maliska surveys the
swiftly decimated meal, the collection of green beer bottles on a
white tablecloth spotted with sweet and sour sauce. He gestures
with the stub of a spring roll, his fingers grey with chalk. "Livin'
large," he pronounces.

Eight o'clock the following morning finds Osman, as
promised, at Sprout's Health Food Cafe, two blocks from his
home. Two framed reproductions of Botticelli hang from the
golden pine walls: *Birth of Venus* and a detail of the central figure
in *Primavera*. (If I were a more serious climber, and placed
routes, I might commandeer the names of select Italian and

Dutch paintings. *Massacre of the Innocents,* with its heavy-metal ring, would certainly go over well in present company. In my case Bruegel's *The Blind Leading the Blind* might be more apropos.) The cafe's menu is inscribed in colored chalk on a black slate: Veggie Crunch; Egg Salad Monster; Ugly Gooey Excellent Nachos. A young woman works behind the pine counter, chopping and milling vegetables for the morning shift. Folkrock issues from corner speakers. Osman is nearly through his Breakfast Burrito—the size of a small loaf of bread—before Maliska and Meeks stride in. Osman and Maliska are regulars, and Maliska flirts with the cook.

Peter Millar soon appears, and joins Osman over coffee.

"Yesterday at the cave," Millar tells him, "it was encouraging to see how much attention you paid to your jump. You really made sure everything was running right. You're not self-destructive. And that's the finest art. If you're going to traverse the edge of danger, the best thing is to remain rational."

Osman nods.

"I saw a lot of people in the Andes," Millar continues. "They were just dumb. They weren't willing to back off in bad conditions. And from a distance you have this radical reputation—your free-solos, your jumps. But in reality you're this really thoughtful person, thinking about what he's doing. It's really good to see."

Osman appears embarrassed by the praise. "Thanks for the acknowledgment," he says.

After breakfast, the climbers discover that Meeks has locked Osman's keys inside the apartment. Maliska offers

Meeks some mild but profane criticism; Osman sighs and pinches his lips. Redeeming himself, Meeks trips the lock with a screwdriver.

We gear up for a morning of vertical ice climbing, and in two trucks drive in tandem to the Spur, an ice-clad crag of metamorphosed conglomerate near Kirkwood, fifteen miles south of Lake Tahoe. We are joined at the site by Millar and Jay Smith.

Described by Osman as his current mentor, Smith, forty-one, is a professional climber and alpine guide. Five feet six and wiry, with a drooping grey mustache and penetrating gaze, Smith says little, smiles less. Osman—who has known Smith for nearly a decade—later praises the elder climber for his stamina and caution as a mountaineer. "If there's anyone who's going to get you to the top, it's Jay. He's solid. But he's not afraid to have the mountain whip him. He's not afraid to back off. He was within two hundred yards of the summit on Everest when his partner's oxygen system failed. His partner urged him to go ahead and tag the top, then come back and join him for the descent, but Jay refused to split up. He did the right thing." Osman pauses. His eyes glimmer; he appears temporarily moved. "Here's a guy, he's been climbing all his life. You know he wanted that summit. He got that close. He may never get another shot. But he turned around."

In the ascent of major peaks via challenging routes, mountaineers or alpine climbers frequently encounter steep, technical sections of hard ice; in order to be passed, such terrain demands fluency with crampons and ice axes. Secured to the boot soles, crampons are metal frames equipped with sharp points for traction on ice and snow. Fluency requires practice, and that, in part, is why these climbers are here. Ice climbing is also practiced as a discipline in its own right; frozen waterfalls are climbed—like most rock climbing routes—not as a means to an end, but for the pleasure and challenge of the climbing itself. At this writing, highly technical "mixed" climbing is in vogue; many of the world's best climbers are seeking and placing routes of extraordinary difficulty over a mixture of ice and rock.

The traditional ice axe averages seventy centimeters in length, from the spike, or steel point at its foot, to the head, which comprises an adze for chopping steps in hard ice and a curved, toothed pick. Ice tools—short-shafted variants of the traditional ice axe—are used, with crampons, to climb steep or vertical ice. Modern mountaineering crampons descend from crude three-point bars, like studded horseshoes, used by alpine shepherds in the Middle Ages. By the nineteenth century, an additional point had materialized. Four-point instep crampons, less substantial than their climbing cousins, are still used by hikers to negotiate flat but icy ground. Having worn instep crampons on a winter descent into the Grand Canyon—layers of perfect snow and burnt-red rock stacked like a tiramisu across the void—on a trail unmaintained and marked only by stone cairns poking here and there through the snow, with one too many sections of solid ice traversing uncomfortable heights, I can attest to the lightweight efficacy of this antique design.

In 1908 British alpinist Oscar Eckenstein added six points to the four, expanding the frame to cover the boot's entire sole.

Initially considered unsporting by many climbers, Eckenstein's ten-point crampons quickly revolutionized the game. Without them, the hobnailed climber had no choice but to chop steps in near-vertical ice with the adze of his ice axe. In 1932 French climber Laurent Grivel added two points to the tip of the crampon; this gave rise to the toe-kicking technique—introduced by the Germans—of ascending vertical or near-vertical ice known as front-pointing. The so-called French technique, developed and long favored by French climbers in the Alps, requires keeping the crampons flat on the ice, bending the ankles and angling the feet away from the slope as the terrain steepens. The French technique is also called *pied à plat,* or "flat-footed." Such technical alpine climbing was born in the French Alps, and French climbing terminology remains in use worldwide. This is particularly true of words describing features of mountainous terrain, such as *couloir* (gully) and *aiguille* (needle, or slender rock spire).

We hike to the base of the Spur and lay out our gear in a dry cave, beside five distinct sections of vertical ice. Of varying breadths, some forty feet in height, the icefalls cling to the shadowed gullies above and descend from the overhanging rock below in the shape of pillars, spirals, or forked tongues. Broadening as they ascend, the blue-tinged masses of clear-water ice are sturdy enough to withstand the blows of ice tools and crampons and support a climber's weight. At their lowermost tips—inches or feet above the snow at the wall's base—they dwindle into icicles the diameter of soda straws. In places, between and behind the bodies of ice, the rock is bare. The conglomerate is much like gravel poured into mortar and allowed to set. Smooth

38

stones the size of eggs may be thumped, loosened, and plucked from its pebbled surface. Here and there, lichen clings to the rock in brilliant shades of orange and green.

Osman, Smith, Maliska, and Millar gear up in crampons and ice tools and free-solo each of the icefalls, one after the other. Meeks remains on the ground, shooting photographs. "Yo, Skippy," Maliska calls to Meeks from overhead. "Hey, Skip," Meeks halfheartedly retorts. This good-natured but derisive exchange has repeated itself throughout the day, and when Maliska descends I ask him the meaning of the term. An experienced white-water rafter and kayaker, Maliska worked for a time as a rafting guide on California's American River. "We called the inexperienced tourists Skippy Flatlander," he explains. "People from Sacramento, mostly. From the flats."

"If you're both Skippies, then," I ask him, nodding at Meeks, "who is the real Skippy Flatlander?"

"We're all Skippies here," Maliska answers, without a trace of irony. "You most of all."

With hundreds of hours of experience on vertical ice, Smith ascends a column with grim, unyielding certainty. When he pauses to examine the route, standing on the front-points of his crampons, he might as well be waiting for a bus. Osman has learned most of what he knows about ice climbing from the older climber. Smith is an adept and willing teacher; while gearing up in the cave, he offered an impromptu primer, largely for my benefit, in the finer points of ascending vertical ice.

With customary aplomb, Osman free-solos a blue helix, spiraling around its core as he ascends. Maliska, watching from the ground, pronounces the route "hairball," a rough synonym of the antiquated "nuts." In this case, the remark is complimentary, closer to "imprudently and stylishly exposed." When Osman has climbed all five icefalls—some of them more than once—he places an anchor and top rope on one of the columns and descends. He offers me a belay, kindly surrendering his crampons and tools to my use. My experience on vertical ice is limited, and I hack skyward, wasting strength with imprecise, unreliable tool and crampon placements, despite Smith's instruction. Near the top, inevitably, I sheer off and hang in my harness. My forearms feel as if they've been flayed. Sweat burns in the corners of my eyes.

Osman offers counsel from below: ascending, I had placed far too much weight on my tools; I need to improve my foot placements, he explains, put more weight on the front-points, and not grip the tools so tightly. After a rest, reinspired, I continue to the anchor and beyond. Relieving Osman of my belay, I practice, unroped, on the off-vertical ice of an adjacent gully. The slope is gentle, but the ice is hard and unforgiving, and I am soloing; a fall would be unpleasant. With little chance of self-arrest, I would likely shoot down the gully, sail through the air, and skip down the crusty slope of snow into the trees.

Later in the afternoon we part ways with Millar, and Osman drops Smith off at his home in nearby Tahoe Paradise. Smith runs an international alpine guiding service out of his home called High and Wild Mountain Guides. A playground of handcrafted training gadgets—designed to isolate the muscles required for rock and ice climbing—stands in his front yard. A dozen down sleeping bags hang like brightly colored cocoons along the rear wall of his modified garage. This, Smith's gear room, is impeccable. Scores of carabiners, cams, stoppers, slings, ice tools, crampons, and other hardware hang in even rows from hooks or lie stacked on wooden workbenches. Coils of rope hang like wreaths from the walls. This is the kind of compulsive attention to detail, I think, that I would hope to find in a partner on a high peak, after an injury, during a storm.

Osman, Maliska, Meeks, and I convoy to South Lake Tahoe and Taco Bell. After the hint of a meal—my bean and cheese burritos are the size and consistency of damp cigars— Osman decides to make a run to Cave Rock for a dusk jump. Maliska and Meeks head directly to the site while Osman stops at his apartment. He hurriedly exchanges ice tools for a rope and climbing gear, and races for the cave against the failing light. On the eastern shore of Lake Tahoe, the cave lies in Nevada. Minutes after crossing the border, Osman is tailed and pulled over by a pair of local deputies. He turns into a 7-Eleven parking lot and produces his license and registration.

He had been traveling sixty-five in a forty-five zone, and his license plates have expired. Worse, his license has been suspended for a missed appearance in traffic court. Osman is under arrest. The climber, eyes downcast, offers not a single word of protest; in his place I argue for leniency. The senior officer is apologetic but unyielding. "If he didn't have a history of no-shows," says the senior officer, "I might let him go."

"I'm so sorry," Osman tells me, and they cuff him.

The two officers search his pockets and truck for contraband. Finding nothing, they put Osman into the back of the four-wheel-drive patrol car. Maliska and Meeks—notified at Cave Rock by another climber who had passed on the road— pull into the 7-Eleven. Maliska waves to Osman and introduces himself to the second officer, shaking his hand. "What happened?" he asks.

"Suspended license," mutters the deputy, a stocky, pale enforcer with little fondness for the likes of the longhaired climbers.

"Don't you hate that?" Maliska asks him.

The officer perches his hands awkwardly on his belt.

"I've never had my license suspended," he answers, "so I couldn't say."

At Osman's request, I place a call to Nanci Nelson and Lennard Glogauer. Retired corporate executives, they live in a three-story home built by Donna Summer in nearby Stateline, Nevada. Maliska, hired as a carpenter by the couple for renovations to the house, brought Osman aboard. Nanci, as she puts it, has since taken Osman under her wing.

"Dan is a great carpenter," she explains. "I got to know him, and realized what a sensitive guy he is, and how people were taking advantage of him because of that. And I started helping him out. There was one lawyer who wanted to represent him, who wanted twenty-five percent of everything he made— even for work he didn't get for Dan. I'm trying to get him started. I've kind of adopted him as one of my kids. He stays in touch. The other day he went out climbing by himself and said, 'If I don't call by nine tonight, call Search and Rescue.' I do worry a lot for him, but I guess that's just Dan. That's his line of work and he thrives on it. What scares me is his jumping. He continues to want to jump farther and farther. I told him, 'You're not getting any younger, Dan. You're going to have to think about your future a little more.' "

Initially intending to impound the truck, the senior officer allows me to drive it to Osman's home. The patrol car disappears with Osman into the darkness.

Meeks, Maliska, and I wait in Osman's apartment and watch climbing videos. "That's hairball," Maliska repeats, offering running and enthusiastic commentary. Meeks, harshly critical despite his intermediate skill, snorts at the efforts of a well-known climber on a 5.13. "He's a geek," he pronounces.

Soon after, Osman appears in the company of Nelson and Glogauer. Osman appears pleased, unfazed by the arrest. Perhaps, because I have such respect for Osman as a climber, I am hesitant to condemn him for what on some level is an inability to function within a bureaucracy. Among his peers, such arrests may indeed contribute to Osman's mystique. This is not unlike the ambivalence one may feel at the excesses of brilliant artists— Picasso's philandering, Faulkner's drunkenness—condemnation or sympathy mixed with some degree of admiration of their inability or refusal to live within ordinary parameters. This, one partially suspects, may be the fate and license of artistic or athletic genius. Osman will free-solo 5.12s, leap with impunity from bridges, speed like a reckless teenager at thirty and disregard the tickets and the courts.

Raised a Pentecostal Christian, Osman has since drifted

from the church. When he prays, he says, which is rarely, it is usually for Emma's welfare. His greatest fear, he says, is to lose his daughter. And while he claims to climb and fall within the limits of his ability, the irony of the fact that he may lose his child by losing his own life prematurely is not lost on him.

"If I fell while soloing I'd go against everything I represent," he says, "which is not pushing it, which is having the route 'in hand.' By dying I would let everybody down—my family, my friends. I'm not trying to create an image, but I can't help but create one. There are people who look up to me, people I may not even know. And I don't want to let them down. I say free-soloing is not a death wish, and then it happens, and people are like 'Hey, you've obviously been talking shit this whole time. What happened? You obviously didn't have that route *in hand.*'

"My daughter will manage," he says, in the event of his accidental death. "She'll be okay." He eschews, at first, the conditional tense. "But I'd be robbing her if I fell. She knows her dad's rad. Other dads don't do this. She's afraid, but she's proud of what I'm doing. It's like my father: I worry about him, getting shot, but then I hear what a good cop he is. And there's a plaque on the wall: Officer of the Year." Osman's expression is a portrait of ambivalence. There is anguish in his eyes, but his jaw is set.

· · ·

On the day of my scheduled fall I wake at four in the morning in the excessive heat of a motel room in Stateline, California, and see Tarver hanging from the rope in the middle of the Utah canyon. The prospect of my jump is terrifying.

Hours later I remain uncommitted as I stand at the edge of the overhanging cliff across the road from Cave Rock, far above the boulders that lie like Galápagos tortoises in eight inches of water on the shore of Lake Tahoe. At a lateral distance from the anchor, I am attached to the cliff by a slender hanging arc of nylon. Higher, on the cliff, Metallica shrieks from the boom box. In context, the music is profoundly unsettling.

Earlier, in the car, I had suggested the possibility of a second rope, a backup, should one fail.

"You could do that," Osman answered. He reflected, weighed his words. "But," he continued with an apologetic grimace, "that's not really what it's about."

He seemed to object to my suggestion not in judgment of my cowardice, which his expression seemed to say was my affair, but in defense of ritual. As if, because he knows a second rope to be superfluous, the aesthetic and thus the spirit of my jump would be defiled.

A layer of mist hangs like a belt above the western shore, bisecting the snow-covered peaks that rise beyond. The lake is vast, an inland sea.

Osman points. "Do you see the rock that looks like a skull?" The large stone is pale, ninety-five feet directly below, the sockets and mouth implied by dark patches of lichen. "That's your landing zone," he says. "Step off and aim for that rock."

"Whatever you do," he continues, "don't jump out. Don't jump out. Don't jump out. If you jump out, you may swing into the cliff."

I ask Osman to check the anchor. I have been married less

than a year, and I doubt the wisdom of this. I question my motives. I question the technology involved. For some reason I do not question Osman. He climbs up, checks the anchor, returns. I feel impelled to thank him, shake his hand. I am lightheaded with fear. My heart pounds. My hands are slick and cold. I ask Maliska to turn off the music. The silence helps, and I continue to breathe. I stand facing the anchor, positioned farther south along the cliff, the outside of my right foot flush with the edge of the precipice.

There, on the edge of the cliff, I meet the Phantom Lord.

In a mutation so swift as to be imperceptible, as if externally compelled, I pass irreversibly through Osman's moment of choice. In the attenuated heartbeats that fall between the moment of commitment and the moment of execution, the pooling fear distills, climaxes, and transmutes. The resistance of the will cracks and dissolves. My body, suddenly unbound, becomes weightless, soars in its position on the rock. My back straightens, my head instinctually rises to the sky. A deep, luxurious passivity imbues my limbs. The oxygen is rich, heavy. I have gained no deeper confidence in the equipment. I have in no way lost the visceral suspicion that I may soon lie mangled on the rocks below. I have simply been relieved of my command.

I count to three and step off the cliff. The sensation of the fall begins at once, without the anticipated poise in space. The shoreline within range of my peripheral vision vaults skyward. The cliffside smears into a blur. The acceleration exceeds all expectation. No dream fall, no gently arcing adolescent cannonball from a high board, has prepared me for the rate of my descent. I am not falling; I have been hurled—spiked, perhaps—with celestial gusto from the sky. I lock my eyes on the skull between my feet. There is a last spasm of panic, a final lashing of the dormant will. I release a long, shapeless cry.

The free fall lasts little longer than two seconds, a mere thirty-five to forty feet before the slack is out. The tension on the harness pulls me gently from my course, directs me south into a long swing of two hundred feet, parallel to the overhanging cliff. I shout obscenely. The sky is full of angels. From across my shoulder I uncoil the remainder of the rope and let it fall. It skims the surface of the water. My hands tremble as I lower myself, still swinging, to the shore. I finally alight and stand upon a stone, freeing the anchor of my weight. Dan Osman calls triumphantly from high upon the cliff. I accepted his temptation. I leapt from the precipice and was upheld.

part
two

At nine-thirty on a cloudless July morning in Meyers, California, seven and a half miles south of Lake Tahoe, Osman is waxing his new truck. He is shirtless, deeply tanned, in mustard climbing shorts and a pair of lightweight hiking shoes. His hair, falling past his shoulders, is secured beneath a black, billed cap worn backward. On the front of the cap is the logo of a climbing rope manufacturer.

A mug of drip coffee, pale with half-and-half, steams on the deck railing at the edge of the driveway. Beside it lies a pack of filter cigarettes and a disposable lighter wrapped in a climbing sticker, its childproof lever disabled with a pair of needle-nosed pliers. Osman began smoking cigarettes for the first time last year, and now smokes a quarter to a half pack per day.

A flame-red 1991 Toyota with nearly 127,000 miles on the engine, his truck is in superb condition. In a corner of its open bed lies a small red toolbox, lashed in place with bungee cord. The bumpers are clean—no Beavis, no Butt-head. Inside the truck's extra-cab, the picture of Osman's daughter is pinned to the carpeted transmission hump—the sole detail inherited from his previous truck. A silver skull earring the size of a pinto bean is pinned to the dashboard; under the pressure of a fingertip, its hinged lower jaw opens and closes.

Osman moves slowly around the body of the truck, polishing the wax to a high shine. Metallica's latest release, "Load," thumps inside the cab. Metallica has apparently softened; some of the cuts on this album—acoustic and melancholy—are closer to folk than heavy metal. Osman has owned the truck for a year and treats it with enough care to draw affectionate mockery from Maliska and other climbers. "Vacuumed your truck yet this morning, Dano?" they inquire. Osman only smiles. Osman is by nature a slow, introspective riser, but this morning he is particularly subdued.

Waylaid by professional obligations, I haven't seen Osman in over a year. Immediately following my jump at Cave Rock, I shouldered my pack, said good-bye to the climbers, and drove home to the Bay Area in a state of bliss. I suffered few if any thoughts. I felt empty, consumed, bored out. As I climbed back up the cliff to the others, it felt as if a part of me had not survived the jump; as if something small and shameful had remained behind. That which is clinging, timid, and self-pitying; that measures, counts, controls; that is arrogant, righteous, and ambitious; that is petty; that fears indifference, humiliation, betrayal, decay—briefly fell away. When I surrendered, the moment before I stepped off the cliff, all of this was torn from me like a scab. It grew back, predictably, in the hours and days that followed, but for a short while I had a glimpse of what it meant to be free.

. . .

||ver the last year Osman has secured a position—an adjunct professorship, officially—as climbing instructor at the local Sierra Nevada College. He has also acquired sponsorships from Timex, Nike, and a handful of additional climbing equipment manufacturers, including Black Diamond and Maxim Ropes. In the spring of 1995, with the help of Maliska and others, he rigged the ropes for the 1995 Eco-Challenge, a multiday race in which teams of five competitors climbed, canyoneered, rafted, canoed, mountain biked, and rode horseback through the canyons and desert of southeastern Utah. His image has continued to appear in television advertisements for banks, footwear, and automobiles.

Most significantly, perhaps, Osman has been recruited to the prestigious North Face climbing team, a collection of the world's foremost rock climbers and alpinists, including Lynn Hill, Jay Smith, Kitty Calhoun, Alex Lowe, Greg Child, and Conrad Anker. In August 1995 Osman joined these and other North Face climbers on a five-week expedition to the Ak-Su Asam-Usen region of Kyrgyzstan, a former Soviet republic. The expedition was a great success—without injury, the team placed five new routes and freed two aid climbs established by the Russians, including the first all-free ascent (a twenty-eight-hour ordeal) of the *Perestroika Crack*, 5.12, on the Russian Tower.

Photographs of the expedition now grace North Face catalogs, magazine advertisements, and posters. A life-size print of Osman climbing in the Ak-Su hangs from the wall behind one of six cash registers at Marin Outdoors, an outdoor clothing and equipment outfitter the size of an airplane hangar, ten minutes from my home near San Francisco. Osman's pose is dynamic, superheroic, and the accompanying text promotes a line of North Face climbing clothing. Not everyone is pleased by such promotion; in recent years, many climbers have begun to complain about the changing face of the sport, about the steady glamorization of a pastime once as marginal—as aggressively peculiar and unfashionable—as computer science.

It is difficult to generalize, of course, but in the sport's so-called Golden Age it would be fair to say that most serious rock climbers were a bright, creative, handy lot. They tended to be mathematically or scientifically inclined. Many were engineers. Some, like Warren Harding, were womanizers and hard drinkers. Others, like Royal Robbins, were chess players, intellectuals. But very nearly all of them, it seems, were fiercely individual, and took a certain pleasure in the fact that rock climbing was arcane, its methods and particularly its motives incomprehensible to ordinary folk.

Now, like the discovery, by developers, of a remote hamlet on a barren rock pile in the south Aegean—a handful of whitewashed shacks, a bar, an absolutely empty beach; a little town you and a few friends found years ago, entirely by accident—the promotion of climbing for profit and as entertainment is viewed by some as nothing short of catastrophic.

. . .

Beneath the kitchen window of Osman's rented one-story, three-bedroom mountain home stand three well-tended rows of pansies and zinnias. The garden is protected by a miniature, plastic picket fence. Nikki Warren, Osman's companion of fifteen months, calls Osman to breakfast through the kitchen window. Warren is twenty-three years old, athletic and striking in the classic, Southern California style. She is five foot ten and a half. Her eyes are a pale, almost lupine blue; her blond hair falls across her lower back. She is dressed in a turquoise running halter, black shorts, and running shoes. A competitive runner, swimmer, and snowboarder, she has been climbing for four years; on a good day, she can lead 5.10.

While Osman eats a stack of pancakes, his plate perched on the edge of a small, cluttered table that serves as desk and dining table, Nikki prepares his lunch: soy cheese and tuna fish sandwiches. On the table, a buxom artificial-syrup bottle stands between stacks of agendas, calendars, climbing stickers, and loose change. The table's second chair is three-legged; the broken front leg lies on the carpet.

Nikki has been up since five-thirty. She wakes every day at that time after five or six hours of sleep and runs six or seven miles or works out in the gym before returning to cook breakfast for Osman and her daughter, Coral Warren, aged six. She is earning a degree as a registered nurse at the South Lake Tahoe Community College. Until recently, she worked three jobs, including thirty hours a week as a clerk at a local sporting goods store—where she met Osman—and thirty hours a week at Sprout's. Osman confesses that he can't keep up with her. Behind her unexpectedly petite voice and perpetual optimism, Nikki is sharp and practical, and her influence on the climber is marked. After breakfast, she questions him about a late bill. He assures her that he paid it in advance, an answer she does not readily accept. When she asks for a check to cover a routine medical expense, Osman signs the check in a near daze. He is feeling the crush of domestic pressure.

At the end of August, the North Face climbing team will gather in the Indian Himalayas to attempt the ascent of Thalay Sagar, a peak in the Garwal Himal range near twenty thousand feet. Osman must decide if he will join the two-month expedition—a rare opportunity for the best of climbers—and sacrifice paying work at home. In addition to his daughter, Emma, Osman now has a new family and the new truck. He is in the hole financially, and he feels it. MTV would like to shoot a paying feature of him climbing and falling in September. Osman has aspirations as a cameraman, and there is work to be had rigging and shooting for a local producer. He continues to work as a part-time carpenter.

There are other factors to be weighed in the decision. Osman is not accustomed to cold, high-altitude climbing and has doubts, given his experience, about the degree of risk involved. Osman also knows that Nikki shares his concerns and would be happier if he remained at home. He has asked her to ask him not to go, even to forbid it, to relieve him of the decision. She does neither, and Osman has been deliberating for weeks.

Nikki's daughter, a talented athlete and able climber at age six, has already top-roped a number of 5.9s. A vegetarian, like her mother, she prefers the taste of soy over cow's milk. After honey and peanut butter pancakes, she turns cartwheels on the living room carpet. Her mother joins her. "One, two, three, go," says Nikki. Together, they vault onto their hands, raise their feet into the air, and hover in handstands until they lose their balance. Coral's and then Nikki's feet touch the floor. "I won," Nikki teases. "Again," commands Coral. "One, two, three, go."

At four feet three inches Coral is the tallest child in her first-grade class. She wears a woman's size 6 shoe. From the sidelines of the soccer field, mothers frequently complain that Coral intimidates their ten-year-olds with her physical, aggressive play. Later, a first-grade classmate spends the night. Although they are the same age, Coral is more than a head taller. Coral's father, a carpenter living in Las Vegas, is six feet four. If Coral maintains her present rate of growth, her pediatrician has predicted her adult height at six feet two.

While her mother works, Coral spends much of her time training in gymnastics and other sports with her aunt Stephanie Warren Hery, twenty, an avid athlete and wife of Olympic gymnastic hopeful George Hery, Jr. Stephanie possesses even more energy than Nikki, if possible, and has Olympian hopes for her niece.

"I went over to Stephanie's," Nikki recalls, "and she was up to her waist in a ditch with a shovel, digging, pulling out rocks. The ditch was full of water. The plumber was leaning in the doorway with his arms crossed. He said, 'If anybody from the shop comes by, I'll never hear the end of this.' "

"He had dug down to the break in the water line," Stephanie explains, "and decided to wait until the city came out and turned off the water. I didn't have anything better to do. My hands were smaller than his; I could reach farther up the broken pipe for rocks."

Osman's breakfast table dominates a small alcove across a cluttered counter from a kitchenette, all open to the wood-raftered living room. A small La-Z-Boy recliner, its brown vinyl upholstery torn, leans against the end of the counter. Along the near wall, beside the sliding glass door to the deck, climbing gear lies scattered in a broad drift. There are three large backpacks, a carton of gymnastic chalk parceled into bricks, rolls of white athletic tape, binoculars, half a dozen pairs of climbing shoes, a wall hammer, racks of carabiners, stoppers (alloy wedges, in varying sizes, to secure in cracks for protection), camming devices, and duffel bags splitting with harnesses, slings, and coiled rope. A mere fraction of Osman's equipment, the assembled gear conceals some thirty square feet of carpet. Elsewhere on the floor is a stuffed, tricolored parrot, a tin of chewing tobacco, a hand towel streaked with red wax. In the corner, beside the brick fireplace, a CD player stands on a stool behind stacks of CDs and cassettes. Predominantly heavy metal, including Metallica, Pantera, Nirvana, Sepultura, Megadeth, White Zombie, Queensrÿche, and Alice in Chains, the collection is leavened with the likes of Enigma and Van Morrison. Four pitons have been driven between the bricks of the fireplace; carabiners dangle from their eyes. Framed photographs of Osman, Nikki, and their daughters, many of them taken while climbing, rest on the mantel. A worn couch stands against the wall beyond the fireplace. Above it, six feet from the floor, a toy helicopter spins slowly from a length of fishing line, pinned to the rafter overhead. A plastic Spider-Man hangs by one hand from one of the helicopter's skids.

In context, the presence of this figure is unsurprising: Spider-Man may be the only climber in popular American mythology. The Web Caster, as he is also known, sprang from the pages of Marvel Comics in 1962 and has maintained a steady popularity ever since. The superhero climbs walls, stands on ceilings, swings from webs, and battles villains, often on the rooftops of his native New York City. Every so often, in the course of recovering some lost artifact of my adolescence, I stumble across my collection of comic books in my parents' sweltering, unventilated attic in northwest Washington, D.C. Spider-Man dominates the collection by a wide margin, followed by Iron Man, the Silver Surfer, and the Fantastic Four. It was in some part under Spider-Man's inspiration that my friends and I began to climb banks, warehouses, and apartment buildings in suburban New York at the age of eleven or twelve. Even from the saddles of our parked bicycles on the corner of Main Street and Broadway, judging the proximity of one building to another, the relative heights of their flat roofs, the routes to their summits, and the lines of sight by which we might be apprehended by authorities on the ground, lent adventure to the lumpish, practical architecture of our small downtown.

Osman, smoking on the deck after breakfast, recounts the story of his first avalanche. With Conrad Anker and Lynn Hill, he was descending a fifty-degree gully in the Ak-Su with ice tools and crampons. The three climbers were unroped. Osman was in the lead, or lowermost position, followed by Anker, then Hill. It was after three o'clock; the afternoon sun had warmed the ice and snow in the gully. Suddenly, a mass of billowing snow roared down on their position. Despite her extraordinary ability on rock, Hill, like Osman, had little experience at high altitude. Anker, who had been climbing aggressively in the high ranges for years, scuttled swiftly on his front-points to the side of the gully, anchored each tool with a vigorous swing, and flattened himself against the ice. Osman followed suit. Hill froze in place, her head back, and watched the avalanche approach. An instant later she was struck and blown from her position. In horror, Osman watched her go by, windmilling with her arms, as the avalanche passed over and around him. Swinging hard with her tools, "swimming," Hill fought to stay on the surface as the avalanche swept down the couloir. When the slide finally came to rest, Hill stood buried to the waist but unhurt, two hundred feet below her companions.

. . .

||*untin' Gators*, 5.12b, ascends from a broad, sloping bench of pale granite streaked with black lichen far above the shores of Emerald Bay, an inlet carved from the southwest shoreline of

Lake Tahoe. Established by Osman himself, the route is short and severe, a jumble of steeply overhanging blocks rising up and out sixty-five feet to an overhanging headwall and the anchors— two hangers fixed to the rock by 3/8-inch bolts. From there, if the climber has the gumption to continue, a finger crack may be followed obliquely up and to the left, forty-five feet to another pair of anchors. The second route is *Drinkin' White Lightning,* 5.12d; climbed in tandem, the two routes together comprise *Cajun Hell,* 5.13a/b.

A route is generally rated according to its most challenging move. If a route is composed of a chain of 5.7 moves broken by a single 5.11 crux, it is rated 5.11. A route composed almost entirely of 5.11 moves may also be rated 5.11—such ratings are often identified in guidebooks as "sustained"—or it may be upgraded to a 5.12 for the endurance it demands.

Today Osman is feeling his age. Six feet from the anchors on *Huntin' Gators,* he fails to execute a 5.10 move for lack of strength. Despite his muscular appearance, he is out of the condition required for such a route. He has been building a custom home in Moab, Utah, for Jay Smith, and this is his first climb in eight weeks. The move requires a standard technique called a lock-off: with his right hand gripping a handhold overhead, Osman must pull his right shoulder to the level of his hand and "lock" the elbow in the closed position, thus acquiring the necessary height for a long reach to the next hold with his left. He establishes the lock-off, but his right biceps fails as he makes the reach. Osman groans. In slow jerks, the angle of his elbow widens until he hangs straight-armed from the hold. He swears.

Calling to his belayer for tension, he moves down and hangs from the last bolt—a practice known as hang-dogging—to rest. Climbers typically hang-dog while working on routes above their ability; it gives their muscles a chance to recuperate while they study the next sequence of moves. Some purists consider hang-dogging poor form, and insist on lowering back down to the ground after a failure before reattempting the route.

Osman placed the bipartite *Cajun Hell* in 1988. For many years the crack of *Drinkin' White Lightning* was believed to be unclimbable. When Jim Bridwell, a renowned climber, rejected popular wisdom and prophesied that the route would "go," or surrender to a first ascent, Osman stormed the crack and solved it in two weeks.

While establishing a new and difficult route, it is not uncommon for a climber to arrive at an apparently insoluble problem—a loose flake, for example, threatening to come off under pressure, without which the route could not be climbed, or a pocket too shallow to provide an adequate grip. Some climbers may spend weeks puzzling over the problem, seeking an alternative route or variation in technique with which they might surmount the obstacle. Failing this, they may abandon the route unfinished. Others will glue, drill, chip, or otherwise edit the offending terrain to "make it go." While common in Europe—especially in southern France—this is generally frowned upon in North America. In one of the most notorious cases, French climber Jean-Marc Troussier created fifteen two-finger pockets with a drill in the placement of *Frank Zappa*, 5.12d. Many climbers refuse to climb such artificial routes. Others, as a form of protest, boycott entire regions where chipping is common-place. Regardless of their actual positions, the better climbers are frequently accused of this practice. Often, the accuser is a frus-trated peer incapable of ascending a recently completed route. Osman has been denounced for chipping both *Slayer* and *Phan-tom Lord*, accusations he flatly denies.

"Nine years ago, I chipped a couple of holds on two routes at the Pie Shop," he confesses. The routes are *Seek and Destroy*, which he never completed and remains unclimbed, and *Dispos-able Heroes*, 5.12c. "I just so much wanted to make them go," he says. "And I admitted it. I told everyone. I wasn't proud of it. Since then, I've removed loose, broken rock from within pock-ets, which in my view is not altering the rock. But I've never chipped another hold." Osman is more tolerant of glue. "If I think a flake is going to come off under the climber's weight, I'll glue it. That's not altering the terrain; it's preserving it in its original form."

Hanging from his belay on *Huntin' Gators*, Osman rests and studies the route. He dips his hands into the chalk bag at his waist against his back, works his fingers thoughtfully into the fine powder. Withdrawing his hands, he lets his arms hang loosely at his sides, shakes them out, flexes his fingers open and closed. Chalk drifts down through the motionless air and flecks the forearms of Osman's belayer, surgeon Roger Rogalski.

Rogalski, whom I met at Cave Rock on my last visit, has a crew cut and a greying mustache. He has the pronounced mus-culature of a weight lifter or middleweight boxer, a relative rarity among climbers who, like Osman, tend toward the lean. Standing barefoot and shirtless on the marbled stone, leaning comfortably from his anchor, he wears fingerless leather belaying gloves, their palms burnished to a shine. His manner is laconic, bemused. With the rope locked off in his belaying device, he waits patiently for Osman to continue.

After several attempts broken by rests, Osman soon passes the difficulty, finishes the climb, and continues along the crack of *Drinkin' White Lightning*. The second climb is more challenging, and Osman rests at every bolt. He finally reaches the top anchors and Rogalski lowers him slowly like a plumb bob to the bench. "Sad," Osman berates himself as he descends. "Sad."

Osman and Rogalski work out on the two climbs for the better part of an hour, alternating belays. Osman warms up, revealing his customary flash. Rogalski is a strong, graceful climber. Aside from the occasional word of advice or encouragement, very little is said. The air is warm and still. A hummingbird floats across the rock face. Weeds grow in spidery patches from the cracks.

Hundreds of feet below, boat traffic scars the wind-rippled surface of Emerald Bay with thumbnails of foam. Cars wind in chains along the road at the cliff's base. It is Sunday, and the bay has the unenviable distinction of being the most photographed body of water in the world. A small, stony island rises from the center of the inlet, crowned by what appear to be the ruins of an abandoned castle. The parking lot at the trail's base is full; drivers wait in idling cars for slots to open. Others have parked beside the road. Osman's truck is parked illegally, wedged between two boulders and a picnic table with only centimeters to spare.

Farther down the sloping granite bench, Geoff Maliska, Jason Kuchnicki, and Aaron Culp work out on *Psycho Roof II*, a 5.12a/b that Osman put up in 1988. With blond, shoulder-length hair and abstract tattoos fading from his forearms, the twenty-five-year-old Kuchnicki is a surveyor and part-time firefighter for the U.S. Forest Service. Culp, twenty-seven, is an apprentice carpenter.

I drop down from Osman's position, higher on the stone bench, and accept Kuchnicki's offer of a belay on the cryptically titled *Phal-lucy*, 5.10d. Culp has already led the climb, and the rope remains clipped to the anchors, ninety feet above the deck. Without a warm-up, I nearly fail on the unfamiliar route; after a difficult start I'm stopped cold by the crux, an awkward high-step surmounting a short, overhanging ledge halfway through the climb. I hang too long on failing forearms and narrowly avoid coming off. I back off the crux and crouch on my heels under the ledge. I breathe, shake out my arms. After a rest, I try again, studying the move more closely. With a different approach I pull it off, just barely, and continue through a gentle section to a second crux. The burn in my forearms is becoming unmanageable, but there is no adequate stance for another rest. I must climb quickly if I'm to finish the route. As I weight the next handhold, shifting my feet, my grip starts to fail, and I prepare to fall.

I'm not coming off, I decide, and tighten my grip. I reach

higher, pinch the next hold, and shift my feet. Again my grip is failing. I'm coming off. I cling desperately to the rock. One more, I tell myself. Just reach for the next hold. And there it is.

Weight on your feet. Keep your weight on your feet. I chalk up unsteadily. One more, I command. Move by move, I creep skyward. Soon the difficulty is past. The climbing softens and I touch the anchors. I gesture to my belayer with satisfaction and stand for a minute in balance, watching the bay, the heat ebbing in my arms.

In recent months, climbing regularly, I have been toproping and bouldering 5.10s and a handful of 5.11s, the most challenging of these in poor style. After an extended siege—numerous attempts spanning a period of months—I am a single move away from "sending," or successfully climbing, my first 5.12—a short problem not far from my home in Marin County, California. The climb lies at the outside edge of my ability, if not beyond it, and the last edgy move—the climb's crux—may not materialize for weeks. A siege may last over days at a time, climbing and flailing and resting and scheming single-mindedly on a particular route.

A climber is not rated by the hardest route he or she has ever climbed—though some climbers at a safe distance from the crags tend to rate themselves in this manner—but by the highest grade at which they can climb consistently, comfortably, on a wide variety of terrains. There are 5.10 slabs—a slab is a gently sloping rock face—and there are 5.10 overhangs. There are 5.10 cracks and 5.10 face-climbs, each requiring a different battery of skills. To crack-climb is to ascend or traverse a fissure that runs through the rock. As the width of the crack varies—from a fingertip to more than a climber's body in width—the technique varies with it. While technically distinct from face-climbing (or climbing through the use of edges, buckets, knobs, and other natural features), crack technique is an equal part of any serious climber's repertoire.

While top-roping, the rope ascends directly from the climber's harness to an anchor at the top of the route, and from there to the belayer. The belayer is positioned above, near the anchor, or more commonly on the ground below. As the climber ascends, the belayer—harnessed to the rope through a belaying device—takes up the slack, maintaining a degree of tension specified by the climber with calls of "slack" or "up-rope." If the climber intends to rest completely on the rope, he or she will call for "tension" or "take." Properly belayed, a top-roped climber will drop no more than a few feet after a fall. The top-rope anchor must be "bomb-proof," or capable of withstanding any conceivable fall. A top-rope anchor is commonly a pair of bolted hangers, a stout tree trunk, or an anchor system comprising at least three pieces of protection, although some climbers insist on four or five. In such cases, the individual pieces are ideally equalized—rigged in such a way that potential loads will be evenly distributed among them.

The traditional lead climber enjoys no such guarantee. With the end of the rope attached to his or her harness by a figure-eight knot or equivalent, the leader climbs with an assortment of quickdraws, carabiners, and protection devices clipped to harness loops, or, more often, to a gear sling worn across the shoulder like a bandoleer. With varying frequency, as the terrain affords, the leader places each piece along the route in sequence, clipping each to the rope with a carabiner. Depending on the route, the leader will also carry a number of runners—nylon loops of varying diameter—to help reduce rope drag. Rope drag increases with the severity of the angles taken by the rope as it winds through the chain of carabiners, as a boot lace crosses back and forth between eyelets. Not merely a question of comfort, poorly managed rope drag can soon arrest a leader's progress entirely. Since optimal placements for protection rarely occur in a straight line, the leader may reduce these angles by clipping runners between each piece of protection and the rope.

While leading, a climber is said to be "on the sharp end of the rope." Given the elasticity, or stretch, of modern nylon climbing rope—which prevents the rope from breaking under the shock of a long fall—a leader who comes off twelve feet above the last piece of protection will plunge more than twenty-four feet before the belayer can arrest the fall. Uncommonly, one or more pieces of protection will fail—almost invariably due to poor placement—under the stress of a long whipper, before the fall is held. In the worst of cases, poorly placed protection will rip out, zippering one piece after another, and the leader may strike the earth or belay ledge in what is known as a ground fall. Colloquially, to strike the ground after a fall is to "crater" or "deck." Leading, then, is technically and psychologically much more demanding than top-roping, and some climbers who top-rope 5.10 or 5.11 may only lead 5.6 or 5.7, if at all. In rating themselves, climbers commonly specify, for example, that they can "lead 5.9, follow 5.11."

Following, also known as seconding, is technically closer to top-roping. After the leader has climbed a "pitch"—a distance of approximately one rope length, or one hundred and fifty to two hundred feet—and arrives at a suitable belay stance near the end of the rope, he or she places a solid, ideally bomb-proof anchor and belays the second climber from above. The second "follows" the same route, removing or "cleaning" the protection during the ascent. As in top-roping, a properly belayed second will usually drop no more than a few feet during a fall, and cleaning protection is generally less taxing than placing it. Thus, climbers of markedly differing ability can climb the same route satisfactorily, the better climber leading every pitch. Well-matched climbers commonly swap leads.

To climb a route for the first time without a single fall is to "flash" it. To do so without prior knowledge of the route (such prior knowledge is called beta) is to flash the climb "on sight." To flash on sight while top-roped is far less significant, of course, than a flash on sight lead, and many climbers would not grace a top-rope with qualifiers. A climber can acquire beta verbally or by watching other climbers on the route. At the Mission Cliffs climbing gym in San Francisco, a young male climber, with a muffled guffaw in the direction of his companions, recently asked the visiting Lynn Hill to sign a poster "To Larry— Thanks for the beta." At five feet one, the soft-spoken Hill might well be the most widely known and universally respected rock climber in the world; her one-day free ascent of the Nose on El Capitan in 1994 is considered the single most impressive climb in the history of the sport, bar none. In context, the request was akin to asking Michael Jordan to sign a basketball: "Thanks for the pointers on my aerial dunk." With a polite smile, Hill signed the poster as requested.

Distinguished from "traditional," or "trad," climbers, so-called sport climbers protect their routes with permanent steel hangers, affixed to the rock with expansion bolts ¼ to ½ inch in diameter. These bolts and hangers—like those placed by Osman and others at Cave Rock—remain in the rock until hammered or drilled out. The traditional climber, on the contrary, favors removable pieces of protection—stoppers, camming units, and the like—placing bolts only *in extremis,* if at all. Once removed from the route, such "clean" protection leaves essentially no trace on the terrain. For sport climbers, intensive bolting is not merely a question of taste; the routes they favor—steeply overhanging, for the most part, with poor opportunities for clean protection— commonly require bolts if they are to be protected at all.

The traditional style is ecologically minded, born of the movement to climb clean that blossomed in North America in the early 1970s. Inspired by the example of Yvon Chouinard, given voice by Doug Robinson in Chouinard's 1972 equipment catalog, the movement arose primarily in response to the devastation of piton scars left in the cracks of Yosemite Valley and elsewhere by climbers of the 1940s, '50s, and '60s.

Many climbers have been around awhile, and remember when climbing was not featured on the likes of ESPN. Many of the old school view modern "sport" climbing as stylistically de-generate and environmentally destructive, to say nothing of overtly *competitive* climbing, an outgrowth antithetical to the spirit of the original game. A few years ago, an East Coast reactionary went on a "mad bolt-chopping rampage," as Osman describes it, through the Western states. He hacked and sledged the bolts from scores of routes, destroying a good deal more natural rock than the bolts themselves.

Despite increasing polarization, there is considerable over-lap between the two camps. While there are some hard-bitten traditionalists who use nothing but clean protection and will never "clip a bolt" (or attach their rope, with a carabiner, to a bolt and hanger), most professedly traditional climbers will drill the odd bolt where common sense requires. Most sport climbers, Osman included, are happy to climb traditionally where terrain affords. Many classic traditional routes (including, ironically, those with piton scars, the indelible wounds of a less enlightened age) are so revered that the appearance of a single new bolt in their proximity would raise cries of outrage from traditional and sport climbers alike.

In the great majority of cases, a sport climber will rappel from above while establishing a new route, drilling each bolt while hanging comfortably in the harness. With bolts in place, the climber will then attempt to work out the moves from below. Long frowned upon by traditionalists, "rap-bolting" requires dramatically less patience—to say nothing of skill—than its al-ternative, ground-up bolting. A strenuous variation closer to traditional than sport climbing, ground-up bolting demands that the climber place each bolt, in order, while leading the route from below.

Ground-up bolting is ethically more sound, given the unwritten policy regarding claim: when a climber identifies a new line at a climbing area, he or she may stake a claim on the route by placing the first, lowermost bolt. Some climbers secure a piece of red tape to the base of the route, indicating "route in progress, please stay off." The ethic dictates that other climbers ascend no farther than the highest existing bolt on a route in progress. Some, out of courtesy, would stay off a route in progress entirely. Osman has had trouble in this regard; other well-known climbers have been discovered actively working on Osman's projects in his absence. To go so far as to place bolts on another climber's route in progress—unless explicitly abandoned by its founder—is perhaps the ultimate transgression among sport climbers. The first climber will certainly remove the invading hardware, and depending on his character, confront the offender. Routes have been stolen in this fashion: building on weeks or months of another climber's work, the newcomer finishes the route and places the last bolts. If uncontested, the climber may name, rate, and report the route as his or her own. Osman has lost at least one route in this manner. In one such case, lest the theft be misconstrued as accidental, the usurper left Osman's last established quickdraw on Osman's doorstep. Without a centralized system of route registration and confirmation—an authoritarian alternative, reeking of bureaucracy—this rising pattern of theft may prove difficult to control.

Osman recently discovered a foreign bolt on the completed

Phantom Lord, the implication being that his own, nearest bolt was improperly placed. Fuming, Osman drilled out the interloping hardware, filled the resulting hole with epoxy, and capped it with a molding of fine gravel to render the blemish invisible.

Firm proponents of the ground-up philosophy argue that rappel bolting in any form is profoundly unsporting, even immoral. An unscrupulous rappel bolter could identify and stitch a half dozen routes in an afternoon without truly being capable of climbing any of them. For the rare ground-up bolter like Osman, on the other hand, establishing each route can take months. While establishing *Phantom Lord*, for example, eight feet above the third bolt on steeply overhanging terrain, Osman took more than fifty falls in the laborious process of drilling the hole and placing the fourth bolt with one hand. It took him two days to place the bolt, a process that would have taken minutes on rappel.

All of this is made more complicated still by those miscreants who pervert decent policies for their own ends, like the climber who arrives at a pristine area and nails a string of first bolts along the base of a clean wall, "claiming" eight or ten potential routes in as many minutes. Available rock is finite, of course, and rapidly diminishing. John Bachar is widely known for chopping bolts placed on rappel. In return, Bachar has been repeatedly threatened, his car vandalized. Osman admires Bachar's intensity—his willingness, as Osman puts it, to make enemies for something he believes in. It was Bachar, Osman claims, who had the greatest influence on his early development as a climber, particularly as a free-soloist. "I studied the way he climbs, his style, his level of concentration, his ethics. I idolized the guy," says Osman. "And a lot of people hated John."

. . .

Returning to the crowded parking lot at Emerald Bay, Osman discovers a warning notice from the parking authorities on his windshield. In two trucks, the five of us drive in tandem to Maliska's home in South Lake Tahoe. Osman drives carefully, one eye on the rearview mirror. He has earned six speeding tickets since buying his new truck—three of them over the course of a single weekend—and is operating once again with a suspended license. If he is stopped for any reason, he will again be arrested. I can hardly criticize. Through my teens and early twenties I totaled one car, beat up several others, and lost thousands of dollars to speeding tickets, all the while considering myself a superb driver thanks to an ill-advised compliment, at eighteen, from the car-racing father of a friend of mine. Nevertheless, I am baffled that Osman, a thirty-three-year-old father, continues to drive in this manner. The physical dangers aside (not a primary concern for the bridge jumper and free-soloist), the sheer financial burden of such a habit is enormous. To spare Osman the risk of another arrest on my watch, I make several offers to drive over the weekend. Each he politely declines.

Over the course of a day's driving in the vicinity of South Lake Tahoe, white and green law enforcement vehicles appear frequently—in our wake, in the oncoming lane, stationed predatively on the side of the road. On Route 50 north of Meyers, a sheriff's Blazer appears in the oncoming lane. Osman breaks a conversation in midsentence. His eyes flick down to his speedometer. The needle is fixed to the fifty-mile-per-hour speed limit. Expressionless, he returns his attention to the road. The opposing driver is clean-cut, square-jawed, his glance concealed by dark lenses. The Blazer passes with a thud of wind. Osman glances back at the speedometer. Not a flicker. He watches the broad white stern of authority recede in his side mirror, and his features soften, almost imperceptibly, with satisfaction.

The two trucks pull into Maliska's driveway, spilling dogs and climbers. Maliska hurls his climbing pack into his open garage. The space is cluttered with sports equipment, power tools, and scrap lumber. It is late afternoon, still warm, and the climbers lean passively against the trucks in a circle in the driveway. They light cigarettes. A climbing conversation starts and dies. Minutes pass. There is nothing, apparently, to do. The dogs settle in the dust. Time slows and appears to stop.

    . . .

In junior high and high school, my adolescent colleagues and I passed countless hours standing or leaning or sitting in this mood, dormant at fifteen as retired Greek fishermen in the sun. At the time, I considered them lifelong friends. In retrospect, I realize, most of us were little more than vague acquaintances, drinking companions and fellow delinquents with nothing in common but a township and a fondness for Molotov cocktails, fashioned from grape juice bottles and siphoned gasoline. We would hurl them down a steep road in town, releasing a dense, curling cloud of black smoke and a rolling sheet of liquid fire nine or ten feet high. On one occasion one of us caught fire—the soaked and flaming cotton plug came loose as he reached back to throw, and the burning fuel ran down his arm and across his back. He dropped to the asphalt, thrashing in the dust, and we kicked and smacked at him to put out the flames. Time and again, we could have burned down the houses on that hill. But no one, by some miracle, was ever hurt.

In the years to follow it would take little more than subtle geographic shifts and the pettiest of betrayals to sever all but a few of these early bonds. At the time, we convened on curbs in front of delicatessens, in parking lots and on porch steps, in cemeteries and on the mossy banks of the Hudson River. We possessed the boundless energy of that age, yet we were drawn to environments of stillness and decay, to the ruins, protected by barbed wire, of exhausted industry. We crawled through holes in chain-link fences to drink in condemned buildings, on the roofs of abandoned warehouses, and in forsaken boatyards littered with the giant, rusted limbs of dead machines. We drank beer, illegally procured, or our parents' liquor, and the world sat still. We had no perception of time as a limited currency; our lives were parceled by the hour, and on such a scale the months uncoiled endlessly before us. One year was far too vast a temporal plain to reckon with; its distant border could not remotely be discerned. Yet we were impatient for the years to pass, to bring us to a time of autonomy, of power. This attitude troubled our elders, as it troubles me now, at thirty. "What are you *doing*," they would demand, "just sitting around like that?" "Just hangin'," we would answer. We were waiting, and waiting seemed perfectly natural.

All the young have promise, and we all believed that promise was enough, that potential was self-realizing. One of us expected to become a professional race car driver. Another planned to move to Los Angeles and start a band. As years passed, some of us lost our nerve—myself among them—and engaged; we went to school or learned a trade. It felt like a kind of defeat, and so it was, but we learned to bend our backs. Some—the proudest of us, the most confident, perhaps—continued to wait. Alcohol and drugs have slowly ravaged them, and now, at thirty, their energy is gone. They fear time now, with the rest of us, but they have no tools. Some of them have moved indoors. Others can still be found on the same suburban porches, or leaning on the trunks of cars, nursing quarts of malt liquor on late summer evenings. They deliver bread for a living, or dish potato salad, or snake sewage lines, and continue to wait. When you drive through town, years later, and roll past them, you force yourself to stop and say hello. There is little to say. They look at the ground, and then up and through you and your new, hot-forged life as if through a curtain of gauze.

·   ·   ·

That evening Osman kneels on the carpet in front of his television and reviews footage of himself and others jumping from the bridge. I have seen similar footage before, in Osman's company, and there are times when such sequences elate me. This evening

I am only dazed. There are those professionals and volunteers who consciously and repetitively risk their lives in public service—and not infrequently lose them—for a worthy cause. Many of them, like Osman, have families to support. Watching the bridge jumping, I am struck for the first time by its profound pointlessness, by the immeasurable *gratuity* of the risk. I feel vaguely sickened by the whoops of excitement off-camera, by Osman's enthusiasm at each take. In one long shot taken from the bridge, Osman's colorful, cartwheeling figure makes contact with his shadow on the ground, plummeting so close to earth before he starts to swing that he strikes tree branches. Kneeling on the carpet, the sight of this thrills him. "Look at that!" he cries, rewinding, advancing frame by frame—again and again—through the moment of impact. Part of me wants to shake him, to shout, "You've got a daughter, man! Wake up!" Part of me just wants to walk away, to get in my car and drive. "Lunatics," I think. "Idiots." I try to remember why I jumped from the cliff at Cave Rock, and the emotion—the extraordinary clarity—that it left me with, but I cannot. And part of me wonders, "What happened? How did I become afraid?"

There are shots of BASE jumpers—parachutists who leap from fixed, terrestrial objects—vaulting from the bridge, and bungee jumpers. The footage was taken on a day when filmmakers and jumpers of all kinds gathered for an orgy of daredeviltry. Shot after shot, jump after jump, variation upon variation: backflips, cartwheels, swan dives. In addition to the core of male climbers, Nikki, Stephanie, and their sister Amy—Maliska's current girlfriend—all take roped falls in excess of 450 feet. In

Osman's company, over the last year, Nikki has made dozens of jumps from various cliffs and spans.

Watching them, I realize that these people are having the times of their lives, and refusing to operate on fear. There hasn't been a serious injury since the death of Bobby Tarver. But if and when one element of this system finally fails—a possibility that even Osman won't deny—who among them will be on the end of the line? Will it be worth it then? If not, how can it possibly be worth it now?

There have already been several mishaps. Osman's brushing of the treetops was dramatic but unintentional. Five more feet of rope stretch—next to nothing over a dynamic climbing rope more than six hundred feet in length—could have killed him. In another incident, an element of Osman's body harness failed on impact, doubling him over with a force that bruised ribs and nearly knocked him unconscious. Such a blow could well have injured his spine or ruptured internal organs. And despite Osman's great care, human error has continued to play a part.

On the morning of Osman's record-breaking birthday jump, Meeks—new to Osman's specialized anchoring system—made a subtle but potentially fatal mistake in reconfiguring the anchor prior to Maliska's jump. Osman, positioned beside Maliska at the launching point, did not traverse the bridge to check the anchor. He had given Meeks clear, simple instructions and the younger climber assured him that he understood. That Maliska was not killed is a testimony to the strength of the equipment.

Despite her faith in Osman, I later ask Nikki if she considers the risks of bridge jumping to be significant.

"Definitely," she answers. "Especially the first time. Even after you've jumped a lot, you still think, 'I'm taking a big risk. There is a chance I'm going to die here. There are a million things that could go wrong.' But you think that with anything you do. I ask myself, 'Are we going over our limits? Or are we staying where we're comfortable?' Is it okay to go slightly beyond your limits, where there's a risk? I think we're all saying, 'Yes, I'll accept that risk.' By doing anything that extreme you're accepting it.

"Sometimes I think, 'Am I being selfish here? Am I neglecting the call of being a mother by jumping?' And I really don't think so, because in everything you do in life you have to take risks. You can't stop yourself from doing things that you're driven to do just because something might go wrong. Something could go wrong in a lot of things in life. And even though this is extreme, and the chances are higher, you have to decide in your heart, 'Okay, I'm going to do this, because I have trust in the equipment, and trust in Dan, and if something goes wrong, then it went wrong.' It's just like anything else.

"While you're on the bridge, you're thinking about the whole: life and death, is it worth it, is it not? As soon as you leave the bridge, your spirit's lifted. You feel no hesitation. You're free from that feeling that follows you every day, that little nagging voice that holds you back. Even in something as simple as running—that voice that says, 'Don't run too hard or you'll fall. Don't exert yourself too much.' On the bridge, there are two people inside you. One is willing to do it, and the other is thinking, 'No, no, no, no, no. There's no way. You are not going to jump off that bridge.' And then you break through. By letting yourself jump off you let go of that inhibition. All of a sudden you're free. You're flying. And you come back up thinking, 'I conquered that voice that says, "You can't do that." Yes I can. I can do anything in life.' "

Osman, for his part, argues that automobiles are far more dangerous than rope jumping. This is the classic and often fallacious refuge of the habitual risk-taker. In this case, there are not nearly enough data for comparison. Over time, I expect that highway driving—per capita, per hour—would produce far fewer fatalities than rope jumping. The consequences of mechanical failure in Osman's system are catastrophic. And as Tarver's death illustrates, there is precious little margin for human error. Regardless of its statistical accuracy, the defense is flawed. Risk of accidental death, after all, is cumulative.

Osman's logic may be unconvincing, but his enthusiasm—and Nikki's—is harder to combat. Later in the evening he tries to bring me back around. Ever since my first jump, across the road from Cave Rock, I have been wrestling with the temptation to jump from the bridge. I have never been drawn to skydiving—perhaps from an irrational fear of planes—or bungee jumping, but jumping off the cliff on Osman's rope was a life experience well worth, by my measure, the technical risk involved. One more, I catch myself thinking. A five-hundred-footer; and then I'll let it go.

"That jump you took at the cave," Osman tells me, "was

much more dangerous than anything we do at the bridge. Jumping a short distance is much harder on the gear." A year ago, I believe I would have done it, but my wife Erin has been expecting since January. Unsurprisingly perhaps, the baby's conception has triggered an unconscious, inexorable reconstruction of my relationship to the mountains, to Osman, to risk. I feel a clear ambivalence about this shift, and vacillate between two selves. At this point, caught in the estuary between a younger, bolder self and the cautious, pondering persona that grows quietly beneath, I am unwilling to commit either way. If welcome, I tell Osman, I will join them on their next trip to the bridge. I will observe the system firsthand, and arrive at a decision then.

Later that night, lying awake in my one-man tent on Osman's lawn, I stare at the tent's roof in the darkness and imagine climbing the girder under the bridge, rigged for a fall. I can see the rope, stretching down and away in a long arc. My heart pounds. There, in the tent, I can feel the Phantom Lord's approach.

• • •

At the age of fifteen I coined a puerile rhyme: "When in doubt, go balls out." It was crude and posturing, but my friends and I were impressed by its message, and tried to live by it. We used it as a pep talk, a mantra to encourage action. It helped us pick up girls, pull off stunts, and live our lives, according to our narrow tastes, more fully. I am embarrassed by that rhyme, in retrospect, but there is no denying that some of the finest moments of my youth were preceded by a silent recitation of those six syllables. And while the phrase itself, as I grew older, fell happily by the wayside, its message—act, act, act despite your fear—has continued to inspire me to the present day. Without the spirit of that phrase, I would not write. I would not climb. I would never have dared to approach, without introduction, the woman who became my wife.

Now, I often think, you're curling up. You have become a worrier. You think you are maturing, but you're only starting to obey your fears.

The elder voice will counter: you delude yourself. Life is not about you. You're nearly thirty years old. You have a wife. You want to be a father. Get over it.

.   .   .

At what point, I try to ask myself objectively, do statistically hazardous, entirely elective pastimes become unethical? Put another way: to what degree, if at all, do we owe our self-preservation to those whom we profess to love, to our emotional and financial dependents? At what point does a dangerous pastime, through its mere practice, constitute betrayal? The question has another half: at what point, through abstinence from highly rewarding but hazardous activities on grounds of social responsibility, do we betray ourselves? If so, and most important: how do we find a balance?

I bought my first motorcycle as a college freshman in Berkeley, California. I liked to ride at night, and would often come back from the city, across the Bay Bridge, at three or four o'clock in the morning. The speedometer pegged at 120, but the tach continued to rise, throttle wide open until the engine red-lined. I didn't know how fast I was going. At that hour, the cars doing 70 were like cartons that someone had left in the middle of the road, and I gently slalomed them, crossing six lanes in broad, floating arcs, shifting my weight in the saddle, rising weightless on the foot pegs, far above the black plain of the bay, the wind and the engine one lone, high note rushing past.

I once rode home from a party dead drunk. I was fine, I believed, if I kept moving; the inertia kept me upright. I lowered the kickstand at red lights. At one light, I lost my balance and dropped the bike to the pavement. I stood there for a while, staring down at it, afraid I was too drunk to pick it up. What an idiot, I think, in retrospect. What an inconceivable idiot.

I had many near accidents and earned many tickets—my license was suspended for a time—but I never went down. At the time, I believed that this had more to do with superior reflexes than sustained good luck. This is an old story. I was too good, I figured, to get killed.

My parents, initially ignorant of the bike's existence, were eventually notified by the Oakland Department of Motor Vehicles. When a flurry of tickets was erroneously forwarded to their address in Washington, D.C., my father, wont to open his children's official mail on grounds of urgency, was livid. Soon after, I received a cautious, informative letter. "Everyone I know," he concluded, "who rode a motorcycle for any length of time, ended up permanently maimed or dead."

Soon after, the bike was stolen and wrecked against an oak at the bottom of the hill, snapping the forks and putting a curve in the frame. I was furious. When the police discovered it and notified me, I dragged the bike back up the hill and kept it on cinder blocks for six months. Now and then, when I came home in the evenings, I would peel off the grey rain cover and sit in the saddle of the ruined machine. In the end, I sold it to a wrecker for a hundred bucks. With regret and a certain relief, I decided not to replace it. Like the end of an affair with a lover whom you suspect might kill you in your sleep, the loss of the bike was a complicated gift.

Two years later, when I took temporary leave of Berkeley for a year in France, I finally bought an antique BMW for six thousand francs. The old bike was a different ride, but at the same hours of the early morning, motoring at easy speeds along the quays of Paris with a warm-bellied passenger, the feeling was very much the same.

I have spoken with many riders who have lost several close friends in motorcycle wrecks over the years. Sport riders, for the most part, on street bikes. In some cases, they have seen these people torn literally to pieces by the forces of collision, or held them as they bled to death in the gravel on the shoulders of canyon roads, or in the center of congested intersections, time at a halt and no sound but a distant siren. In some cases, they have delivered the farewells of these friends to parents, wives, and children. They ride their motorcycles to the funerals that follow, often in procession. Many of the surviving riders have gone down themselves more than once, and walk with pronounced limps. Steel pins hold their knees and ankles and wrists together, and knotted scars run along their legs and forearms. They are no longer children, as I was at Berkeley, and they ride with a perfect understanding of the odds. They go to work, and take care of their families, and continue to ride. They get together, often on Sundays, and ride in the hills. They ride not to court an early death, but because when they are not in the saddles of their machines they are only half alive.

A year after I returned from France my own attitude toward motorcycles was tempered by an experience on the California-Oregon border. Shortly after graduating from Berkeley, I drove north to the American Alpine Institute in Bellingham, Washington, for training in glacier travel and crevasse rescue. There was diving to be had as well, in Puget Sound and points south, and the trunk of my car was full of gear: regulators, fins, harnesses, ropes, boots, carabiners.

I had been running out of gas a lot that spring. At first by accident, I soon realized that I found this petty gamble satisfying. I knew it was bad for the car. But when the engine started to cough and stall, my pulse would quicken. Will I make it to the next gas, I'd think, before it quits? Twice in as many months, sputtering along on fumes, the car stalled for the last time within sight of a gas station—the perfect outcome—and coasted in neutral to the pump. It was a game, I thought, and a harmless one. When it died in the middle of nowhere, I'd take the empty red can out of the trunk and hitch to the next town. I'd get dropped off at the station, buy a couple of gallons, and walk back a few miles in the dusk. When I pulled back onto the road, the inside of the car would smell pleasantly of gas from my hands. I would pass the landmarks I had seen already twice, from both directions. These strange towns would seem familiar, and the eight quarts in the tank would fill me with a sense of abundance.

En route to Bellingham, as I rolled through Eureka, California, with the needle in the red, past the Texaco, I glanced at the open atlas on the passenger seat and figured it was worth a shot. Maybe I could get across the Oregon border. By the time I started to doubt it, the heat of the day had broken and long shadows cooled the road.

A motorcycle came up behind me. It eased back and forth in my mirror, then pulled out in a patch of straightaway and passed on the double yellow. The rider was bearded, with bare arms under a denim vest. The bike was a Japanese cruiser, a poor man's Harley. Clinging to the biker's waist was a tiny, sharp-boned woman in a lavender sweatshirt and jeans. Neither of them wore a helmet. They leaned back into the right lane and went over the white line onto the shoulder. The bike slithered in the sand. I started to brake and moved out across the yellow line. The bike eased back off the shoulder, wobbling, and the rider gunned it. The machine shot forward, the sound of the engine crashing off the rock wall that climbed up along the other side of the road.

When I came around the next bend, the biker had reached an inside curve. He had too much speed going into the turn. My foot moved again to the brake. Sparks leapt as the bike's frame touched the asphalt. The bike jerked upright for an instant, the riders' heads bobbing in the air, then plunged back into the rail. The frame dug into the blacktop and the bike's rear end came up off the road like the arm of a catapult. Mysteriously, the bike didn't follow its line of inertia away from the rail, into the open. It clung to the inside as it tumbled end over end, interminably, mashing against the steel railing. Until the end, neither of the riders came clear. My car came to a stop at the same time the bike took its last bounce, finally breaking away from the rail and teetering in a pirouette near the middle of the road before collapsing, rocking still. The bodies lay in its wake, one beyond the other, along the rail. I held the wheel, catching my breath. Let her live, I thought. Let one of them live. After a moment, incredibly, the man rolled over onto his stomach and stood up. His face and arms were slick with gore. He stumbled back up the road to his companion.

"Get up!" he roared, spitting blood. He fell heavily to one knee and jerked her miniature body off the asphalt. She roused and clutched at him vaguely with one hand. He shook her.

"Ow," she yelled. "Don't."

I stared at them through the windshield. The man released her and she began to circle him, bent at the waist, cradling her arm. A dark, bloody handprint lay across the arm of her sweatshirt.

"I knew that was going to happen," she whimpered. "I knew that was going to happen." She repeated the phrase over and over. The arm she carried was grotesquely bent between her wrist and elbow, as if additionally jointed. The man watched her walk in circles around him. He stared at the tattered palms of his hands. "Shit!" he howled. "Shit!"

I leapt out of the car and took several steps toward them, holding out my hand. "Hey," I said. "Take it easy. Here, lean against the railing."

They followed this direction and stared sullenly back at me. The air about them reeked of bourbon.

"I think my arm's busted," the woman said, glancing sheepishly at the disfigured limb. "I told him," she said. "I told him that was going to happen."

"Shit!" the man repeated. His tongue moved in the front of his mouth, working at a tooth. He reached up with his fingers, pulled it from the gum, and flicked it away. He spat a mouthful of blood onto the asphalt, splashing the cuffs of my jeans.

"Are you all right?" I asked them suddenly.

There was a pause. I was as stunned by the question as they were.

"Of course we're not fucking all right, man!" the rider bellowed. "What the *fuck* do you think?" Blood flicked like spittle on the consonants. A droplet struck my wrist.

My God, I thought. I'm useless.

The man looked back at his machine, lying on its side in a pool of gas and oil. Shards of glass and plastic lay along the road in its path.

"I'm going to pick up the bike," he shouted with a note of triumph.

"Yeah, pick it up," cried the woman with the same enthusiasm, as if this were a solution to their problem. The man staggered over to the fallen machine and pulled it off the road onto its kickstand. He tried the electric starter—nothing.

"I wouldn't do that," I said dazedly. "You don't want a spark."

The woman started to cry. "My arm really hurts. It really hurts." She was panting. The man stumbled back and stood beside her. The bike fell back over with a crunch.

"Where else do you hurt?" I asked the woman, edging closer. Dark blue marks had appeared on her forehead. Her skin was turning grey.

"Everywhere," she said faintly. "All over."

The biker stared at her. Unsteadily, he reached out and touched one of her bruises. He left a spot of blood on her face.

"I'll drive to the next phone," I said. "I'll call an ambulance."

The man looked up at me helplessly. The belligerence, the wild disbelief, were gone. He wagged his head. "Go on, man! Go!"

I started the car and drove around the bike in the middle of the road. I was closer to the Oregon border than Eureka— that much I knew. If only somebody would pass by, in either direction; anyone with a full tank of gas. Before I rounded the next curve I glanced into the mirror. The woman had sagged to the ground, her head on her knees. The man stood over her, wildly waving his arm, waving me on.

I coasted on downgrades. I talked to the car, encouraging

it. Three miles down the road I came upon the sign for a camp-site. A ranger station, I thought. Relief hit me in a wash. But there was nothing, no one; just a lot by the side of the river, a grove of trees, five tables in the shade. No phone. I drove on. Two miles later, another barren camp. My hands were damp with sweat. I wiped them repeatedly on the legs of my jeans. My pulse choked me, filled my head, drummed in my legs, coursed down my arms into my fingertips. I took long breaths. I stared at the needle on the gas gauge, resting on the peg, for a flicker of motion. I watched the odometer turn. Seven-tenths, eight-tenths, nine-tenths, eleven miles. One-tenth, two-tenths, three-tenths. At the twelve-mile mark I came around a curve and saw the Oregon State Line Inspection Station. I shouted, pounding the dash.

When the man in the uniform had made the call for the ambulance, I asked how far it was to the next gas. Another five miles, he said, most of it downhill. I crept north. Loose now, coming down, the sweat lay cold on my skin. My heart was walking it off, soft and booming, like the quiet unraveling after a fight. Hooohh, I kept breathing, shaking my head. Hoooohhh. The car stalled twice a mile or so out of town. Each time I waited, coasted, started it again, and got a little more. The third time, coming out of the hills and past the first houses, the engine refused to turn over. I turned off the ignition and rolled down the road in neutral, engine silent. Three boys on skateboards stopped and watched me glide by, tires whispering on the asphalt. The road flattened out and I began to lose speed. A sign for gas finally appeared. I crossed the oncoming lane, trundled through a rain puddle, and with the gentlest touch of the brake came to a stop at the island. As I stepped from the car an ambulance flew past, lights flashing, heading south.

The station was closed, the proprietor gone. I had missed it by twelve minutes, and the sign said it wouldn't open until seven the next morning. I looked at the map. Not far to the north lay a substantial town. I found my dive knife in the trunk and walked around the abandoned station, searching for a hose to siphon gas. Several cars, some on blocks, rested like buffalo in the high grass behind the station. Beyond a row of pines lay trailers. Country music drifted faintly through the trees.

Beside the station, a black Lab dozed beneath a pine. A long piece of frayed rope was tied to its neck, the end chewed through. The dog's fur was pale with dust. Flies moved across its ribs. I crouched down. The dog woke up, cocked its head, smelled my hand. I cut off the rope.

Across the road stood a bar. I pulled the red can from the trunk. I took two singles out of my wallet and a dollar in change from the ashtray. I stuffed the three dollars into my pocket, tucked the wallet under the seat, and locked the car. Eight or nine cars and trucks were parked in front of the bar. Inside, it was dark and cool. Garth Brooks played on a brand-new juke-box.

A woman in her thirties was clearing a pool table, a cigarette loose in her mouth. She bent at the waist, tilted her head away from the smoke, and made her shot—a powerful, controlled stroke, the tip of the cue following through, up and away from the table. Two stripes went down like rifle shots. She studied the table impassively, flicked her ash. The cue ball finally came to rest against the rail. Her opponent leaned against a stool, clasped the point of his cue, and rested his chin on his hands. Another woman laughed, took a hit from a green bottle. I approached the bar. "Hey," I said, nodding.

"Hey," said the bartender flatly. His tongue played with a toothpick in the corner of his mouth.

"Outta gas," I said, lifting the can into his line of sight. "I missed the station by five minutes." I nodded at the wall facing the street.

"They don't open till morning," said the bartender. He pulled his cowboy boot up onto the edge of the ice well and leaned his forearms on his knee, his long, venous hands hanging loose.

"Yeah," I said. "I was hoping to find somebody here to sell me a gallon or two, just to get to the next gas."

The bartender called down the bar, over the music.

"Bill, you got any gas for this fella?"

Bill was short and stocky, his skin pale. He wiped the moisture from a neat mustache the length of his lip.

"How much do you need?" he asked as I approached. He wore shorts and a tank top. His left leg was drawn up over his right, the calf and shin covered with circular, blistered scars the diameter of fingertips. I held up the can. "A gallon, if you can spare it," I said.

"I can spare it," he said. "I'll just finish this."

There was a silence as he drank his beer. He lit a white-filtered cigarette.

"A guy and his girlfriend just went down on their bike a few miles south of here," I told him. "No helmets."

Bill picked his nose with his little finger, flicked it between his knees.

"I've never seen anything like it," I continued. "They went down right in front of me."

"Lucky for you," he said. I glanced at the pool table. The woman was racking.

"Pretty bad, were they?" asked Bill.

"Hard to say," I said. "Maybe."

"Kid last week broke his neck right out here," he said, gesturing to the road with his cigarette. "Suzuki GSX-R 750, boy, right off the fuckin' lot. Heh!" He smacked the bar with his free hand and took a drink. I put the gas can on a stool.

"Local boy," he said. "Hit the speed bump in front of the school at ninety plus. Bounced once and hit the wall. Snap." He tilted his head, cracking the vertebrae with a pop. "His parents sold the bike for fifty bucks. It needed a little work, but shit, it still ran. Guy who bought it rode it home."

He paused, shook his head, and took a drink of beer.

"Fifty bucks," he said. "Ma and Pop didn't know, you know? How're *they* supposed to figure the little bastard saved up six or seven grand?"

He finished the beer and took a long drag on his cigarette.

"Watch this," he said, exhaling, and twisted the butt into

his calf. There was a sizzle and the cigarette went out. A drop of clear fluid trickled down his leg. When he pulled the butt away, the ash left a black ring in the center of the opened blister.

"I went down myself six months ago," Bill said. "Wasn't going that fast. Little Honda 350. Now I got no feeling below the knee." He laughed bitterly and lit another cigarette. "Doctor says the marrow's dyin'. The whole leg's gonna come off in a couple of months." He made a chopping motion against his thigh, near the hip. "I figure why not use it as an ashtray while I got it."

When we had siphoned the gas from Bill's truck, I thanked him and offered the three bucks from my pocket. "I normally wouldn't accept it," said Bill. "But tonight I'm going to have another beer."

.   .   .

A car door slamming woke me the next morning, just after dawn. I had parked in the lot behind a motel and slept in the car, the seat leaned back, the keys in the ignition.

After breakfast in Grant's Pass I passed a shop with a Diver Down flag in the window. I turned around and parked. The owner rented me two tanks and gave me directions to a nearby river with a falls.

"It's about an hour or so down a pretty bad road," said the owner. "You got four-wheel drive?" I shook my head.

"Well, it's easier to get in than out," said the owner, "so don't push it."

I put the tanks in the trunk and wedged towels and fins

between them to keep them from rolling. Then I drove back out of town the way I had come. A bank sign said 11:02 A.M. Ninety-eight degrees. After almost an hour and a half on the dirt road, following the diver's directions, I crossed the river on a narrow wooden bridge and parked.

By that time, the air was so hot that it was hard to breathe. I went down to the water and took off my jeans. I rinsed the dried blood out of the cuffs, weighted them with a stone, and left them to soak. The water was ice-cold. I geared up, I walked into the river with my fins in one hand and floated, dunking my head. The current barely moved. The water was dark. Trees and heavy brush lined the banks. Upstream tall stones formed a canyon.

I pulled on my fins and kicked easily against the current, lying on my back. Then I put my mask on and rolled over. Snorkeling, I kicked on the surface until I reached the beginning of the canyon. There, in the narrows, the water moved faster. I kicked harder to keep pace, checked my gauges, and descended. As I sank I continued upstream. The canyon walls, grey and luminous, closed in around me. I ran my gloved hands along the polished stone. There were places where the walls lunged out, formed ledges. I passed beneath them, swimming toward the light beyond. Caverns opened up to either side. I went deeper. I found my flashlight with my hand and switched it on, sweeping it into the blackness as I dropped.

I came to a nest of deadfall. Massive, splintered trees like the prows of longships—frozen dragons, mouths agape. Under and over I snaked through. Finally, the tank scraped gently and stopped me. I eased back, surrendering to the current. Something caught and held me, digging like a finger in my ribs. I felt the branch with my hand, tried unsuccessfully to break it. I paused, breathed. Releasing the branch, I let myself go limp. When I had completely relaxed, the current shifted me slightly in the notch. The pressure overhead seemed to ease. I exhaled, gave a gentle kick, and slipped through. Beyond the deadfall the canyon widened. I followed the stone bottom as it climbed out of the darkness, toward the sun.

A froth of bubbles glittered near the bank above. I ascended slowly and found a school of young trout feeding in the mouth of a brook that entered the river. I swam up the brook until I lay in a foot of clear, rushing water. I held myself in place with my hands at my sides, bracing with splayed fingers. The trout ignored me, finning briskly to either side. I tried to discern what they were eating, without success. The small round stones that lined the brook shimmered like amber beads. When I began to get too warm in the sun, I slipped downstream, not lifting my head from the water. I drifted back down to the river bottom and continued on. Soon I could hear the rumble of the falls. The current quickened as the river narrowed. I kicked faster. The bottom climbed steadily. The sound grew louder, a hammering roar. When I came within sight of the falls, I climbed hand over hand along the bottom through the rushing current. I slipped down into a great bowl carved into the stone by the river. At the bottom of the bowl the water was clear and still. I rolled over onto my back.

The sound of the falls filled the bowl utterly like the voices of a crowd of people filling a stone church. I lay on my back in the midst of the sound and watched the mass of water plunge in fierce, frothing heads that lost momentum in the same place and were swept away like storm clouds, out of the bowl and downstream. I reached up and felt the very bottom of the falls in the cup of my hands. There, the water only jostled, bubbles swarming between my fingers. The regulator resisted slightly as I inhaled. When I breathed again, it fought a little harder. I lowered my hands and retrieved the pressure gauge. Nearly empty. I lay on my back, eyes half closed, and watched the rushing water. Down that rutted road, up that river, at the bottom of that wild falls, I felt as far from the world, and everyone in it, as I had ever been. Right then, that was exactly where I wanted to be. Just another minute, I thought, and held my breath.

. . .

At this time in my life, a watershed of sorts, I am unwilling to ride a motorcycle on the street. I so abused the generosity of the Fates that I now fear them as a penniless gambler fears his creditors. I have outstanding debts in this regard, and with a child on the way, I cannot afford to pay them.

Until recently, I never realized to what degree the middle class is a moral, rather than an economic, entity, based less on status than on possessive, life-sustaining love. The moral middle class plays life by percentages, because that is the safest bet, and percentage play—in life as in tennis—is by definition conservative. It is, ironically, the gambler's game. For all appearances, a true gambler never makes a poor bet. He never goes for the long shot. If he is a professional, he always bets the sure thing, and even then he occasionally loses. When the currency in question is your family's welfare, there appears to be no other way. There is a deepening to this kind of life, informed by what the Japanese call *yugen*. An emotion akin to nostalgia, *yugen* might be experienced—as philosopher Alan Watts put it—in an empty banquet hall the day after a wedding. Napkins lie beneath the chairs, the rice crunches underfoot, but the music and the bride and groom and all the guests are gone. The Japanese compare *yugen* to the sight of a ship's sails slowly disappearing around a distant headland, or of geese, in formation, flying into mist. Living a life based essentially upon the protection and preservation of your family is to pit yourself against an enemy—the nature of all things to change and vanish—that you cannot possibly defeat. This is a rich conundrum, offering its own rewards. But it's not nearly as much *fun*, I'm discovering, as riding a Kawasaki GPz at 120 miles per hour across the Bay Bridge at three o'clock in the morning.

I still consider buying a bike for the track, a high-performance street-illegal machine with no license plates and fat, slick tires as tacky in the heat as licorice. I would drive it to the track on a trailer and pay by the hour to ride. A track is blessedly free of obstructions, and the chance of serious injury or death after a fall is infinitesimal. In full leathers and a new helmet, on a clean, beveled track—free of oil, sand, black ice, potholes, mufflers, telephone poles, reckless pedestrians, and desperate, clinging fathers in Volvo station wagons—I could still allow myself to wind it out. And yet, without the terrible, ambient risk, I wonder, would the enormous speed and the wonderful rhythm of the corners all too soon become monotonous? As I slowed and left the track and rolled the bike onto the trailer, while I lashed it into place for the drive home, to my wife, to my future child, would I feel as I've begun to feel now, in Osman's company? That I have changed, that another calling—that of family—has waylaid me, that I am equal to its tasks, that I perform my duty, but that I have chewed through my own entrails to do so, that I am no longer, in some essential way, entirely alive?

This is a paltry price to pay, I answer daily, for a wife beyond all expectation, and for the child she carries—a nameless, genderless child who illuminates the way before us like a brazier. Eventually, perhaps, these vestigial adolescent twinges will subside. I would trade everything I had at twenty again and again for my life now, at thirty. Like the lobsters I used to drag from caves on the floor of the Pacific—wise, ageless creatures, how they fought and fought until they finally surrendered, all at once, and went limp in the hand—I am molting, I hope, into a better form.

Early in my wife's pregnancy, I was top-roping a 5.10 in a climbing gym near our hometown of San Anselmo. I reached the gentle overhang, prepared to move through it—I had climbed the route successfully before—and unexpectedly froze in place. I thought of the baby. The music, cycled perpetually through the gym's loudspeakers, overwhelmed me. I glanced down at my belayer. Her belay appeared sound, but she was chatting with her neighbor, her eyes averted from the route. My motivation to ascend evaporated. The strength drained from my arms. My position—clutching like a salamander to misshapen plastic knobs bolted to a sheet of painted, artificially textured plywood—struck me as absurd. My fear unraveled quickly into panic. I lost all faith in the anchor, the rope, my harness, my belayer, and my ability to climb; I wanted down. I called to my belayer, trying to conceal my alarm, to watch me. I decided to attempt the down-climb, rather than rely on the gear. Clinging to each hold, I descended in horrible, contracted form to the gravel floor.

Sixty feet beneath the surface of the Pacific, alone, I once became trapped in a cave. I started in slowly, rounded a bend, and saw a distant light. Imagining a second entrance, I continued. It was a tight fit; in places, my chest in the sand, my scuba tank scraped against the irregular rock ceiling overhead. When I finally reached it, the opposing aperture was the diameter of a porthole. It struck me then that I might have made a bad decision. With my arms outstretched before me, pushing with bridged fingers, I scuttled backward down the winding corridor. I made steady progress until I stopped short with a thump. I exhaled completely, flattening myself onto the floor of the cave, and pushed again, without result. Just how long have I been down? I wondered. How much air do I have left? My console—equipped with depth and pressure gauges, compass, and computer—was tucked into my vest out of reach; I last checked my gauges before I entered the cave.

I knew the sensation of pulling on an empty tank—we had simulated it in training. The resistance from the regulator stiffens until, at some point in the middle of your last, labored breath, it freezes solid. The valve shuts down and the airspace in the regulator becomes a vacuum; it's like trying to breathe from an empty soda bottle. As a diver, I have often wondered what it would feel like to drown beneath the surface. There, in the cave, I remembered the sensation of the regulator going stiff, stopping, and a wave of claustrophobic terror rose before me. I wanted to bellow, to thrash. An instructor had once observed that panic was a behavior, not an emotion. That it was not fear that killed the trapped or disoriented individual, but the behavior of uncontrolled panic in response. I lay motionless for a moment on the floor of the cave and closed my eyes. I relaxed my limbs completely, and in three breaths the impulse to struggle had passed. I thought the problem through: the flat boot of the tank had caught on an edge that now held me like a barb. I slowly rolled to the left, sliding gently forward and back with my hands, scraping and tapping with the boot of the tank along the rocky obstruction behind me, searching for a slot. No luck. I repeated this process to the right without success. I'm screwed, I thought, and another spasm of fear clutched my chest. I took two huge gulps of air. Think, I commanded. Don't move. Just think. I lay still in the cave until I was breathing evenly, and could no longer feel my heart.

Normally, you could pass such a squeeze by shedding the scuba tank and pulling it along behind you, the regulator secure in your mouth. The passage, in this case, was far too narrow to remove the tank; at first I doubted if I could even work a hand down to feel the obstruction. With a series of contortions I did manage this, and with my right hand I examined the problem.

The tank, slightly buoyant and therefore gently elevated at the boot, angled upward just enough to catch a broad flange of rock. By grasping the foot of the tank and drawing it tight against my lower back, then rolling slightly to the right and exhaling while I pushed off with my left hand, I worked the tank under the lip and scraped slowly under the obstruction. I was soon clear of the squeeze, and the remainder of the passage offered no difficulty. As I backed out of the cave, into the light, I checked my gauges. Two hundred pounds; three hundred pounds below the pressure at which divers are encouraged to surface, but enough. I was free, more pleased by my victory over fear than my escape from a drowning death at the age of twenty-two.

In the climbing gym, however, I had lost composure. Worse, given the circumstances, the fear was unjustified. At the base of the route I untied from the rope, mumbled something to my belayer, and excused myself. I sat in my car in the parking lot, in the darkness, and wondered, melodramatically, if I would ever climb again.

In the gym you can climb more vertical feet in an hour than you might in a long day at the crags. At the gym there is no hike in from the car, no rope to flake (or uncoil), no hardware to rack, no anchors to place. With a belayer, you simply tie in to the rope and go. Fueled by the music—commonly a blend of traditional and alternative rock—the tempo is quick, the climbing aggressive. Most traditional climbers resort to the gym only when forced, by darkness or poor weather, if at all. But there is a new breed of climber, introduced to the sport in the gym, that climbs exclusively indoors. This individual has never climbed on natural rock, regardless of local availability, and has little or no intention of doing so. There are surfers, I imagine, or will be, who live within a reasonable drive of decent, oceanic surf who have never caught a wave outside a wave pool. No sharks, they might argue. The perfect, consistent wave. Twelve minutes from work. A locker room. *A juice bar.* All too soon, there will be a climbing gym in Yosemite Valley—like a neon wedding chapel erected in the center of the nave of Saint Peter's—and they will pack it in.

Sitting in the car, I unwound the strips of white athletic tape from my fingers. The tape, wrapped around the soft pads between the knuckles, supports the tendons. I rubbed the streaks of residual glue from my ring finger. From my wallet, tucked above the visor, I extracted and replaced my wedding ring. I studied the band of white gold, plain as silver in the light of the streetlamps, and drove slowly home.

For practical reasons, I do not climb wearing the ring; it would interfere with my grip, and could become dangerously wedged in cracks. The soft metal would be damaged, particularly on natural rock. It was a difficult decision, the first time I went climbing after the wedding. I considered taping over it, to protect the metal, but this posed its own problems. Glue would foul the ring, and the resulting lump would be even more awkward than the ring itself. At first, I wore the ring on a chain around my neck, tucked under my shirt. I soon became afraid of the chain breaking, perhaps in a fall, and of losing the ring forever. Thereafter I strung the ring on my leather watchband and stashed it deep in a pack pocket, or tucked it into the furthest corner of my wallet. Taking it off and putting it back on became a minor ritual. I would study the appearance of my hand in contrast. With ring. Without ring. Removing it, I continue to feel a faint pang of endangerment, as if I am colluding with chaos; seeing it again in its place is as satisfying to the eye as a tarnished copper kettle, its brilliance surfacing beneath the labor of a polishing hand. And yet the ring—or what it represents—is heavy; it gives weight.

After a week of inactivity and self-loathing, I continued to climb, but with greater caution. I drove with circumspection. I pondered life insurance. I took up tennis.

As I clung to that overhang and imagined the baby, still small enough then to fit in my closed palm, I felt painfully exposed. In the minute, infinitely fragile fetus, I perceived the frailty of things—myself included—in a way I never had before. Furthermore, I suspected, with the confirmation of this life *in utero*, my personal exemption from disaster had expired. My luck was up, and the angels had diverted their attentions to the child. They had preserved me through my youth for this transmission; through conception I had passed them on. Get down, said a voice. Get down. There is danger here, and it does not serve.

· · ·

The morning after Osman's trip to Emerald Bay, Nikki rises at five-thirty and goes for a six-mile run. Osman, still groggy at nine-thirty, nurses a mug of coffee on the deck. Coral eats raw cauliflower and turns handstands on the carpet. An MTV director calls to discuss an upcoming shoot featuring one of Osman's falls. The climber proposes a fifty-foot jump at the nearby Mayhem wall. The location is more telegenic, Osman argues politely, than the site favored by the show's producer. "Maybe," the director tells him, "but she really wants a longer fall." The producer doesn't want an attractive canvas behind a token drop. This is MTV, after all, in *New York*—and she wants the Big Air. After the conversation Osman hangs up, sighs, and retires to the deck for another cigarette.

Osman and Maliska had planned on an "El Cap day" at Lovers' Leap, eighteen miles south of Lake Tahoe on Route 50. The Leap is a granite wall, one-quarter mile long and ranging in height from 350 to 600 feet. Legend dictates that the cliff is named for a pair of Indian lovers; thwarted in their desire to marry, they jumped together to their deaths from the stony bluff. An El Cap day involves climbing over 3,000 vertical feet— scaling a 150-foot wall twenty times, for example—in one period of daylight. The exercise takes its name from El Capitan in Yosemite Valley, the highest vertical wall in North America. The longest route up the face of El Capitan, the Nose, is more than 3,000 vertical feet—some thirty-five pitches—and commonly takes three days to ascend.

Maliska appears at one-thirty in the afternoon, parking his pickup on the street. He leaves both doors of his truck open, heavy metal pounding from the cab. After half an hour of casual deliberation, Maliska decides that it's too late in the afternoon for an El Cap day and departs; weeks of overdue yard work await him at home.

Instead, Osman and I join Coral, Nikki, and Nikki's

mother, Cynthia Warren, forty-five, for a less ambitious outing to the same site. With a partner, Cynthia recently ascended the seven-pitch *Snake's Dike*, 5.7, up the flank of Yosemite's Half Dome.

At the base of Lovers' Leap, Osman sets a top rope for the Warrens on the first pitch of *Fantasia*, 5.8. Coral discovers that she has outgrown her month-old rock climbing shoes. With her mother belaying, she ropes up and climbs the first pitch of *Fantasia* barefoot. Osman and I continue along the trail, following the base of the cliff. At the foot of *East Crack*, 5.8, we encounter an acquaintance of Osman's, belaying a partner overhead. The climber is despondent: his pack and all of his climbing gear—worth hundreds or thousands of dollars—have just been stolen from his tent at the Lovers' Leap campsite. Furthermore, he explains, he recently became a father against his will and is being sued for child support. I ask if the relationship with the child's mother is salvageable.

"Salvageable?" he raises his voice. "There *is* no relationship. I called her the other day and she told me, 'You don't fucking know shit.' That's what she said: 'You don't fucking know shit.' There's nothing to salvage. She's destroying my life." He glances up at his partner; the climber is securing himself to a ledge.

"I hate this country," he says finally.

Osman and I continue to the base of *Bear's Reach*, 5.7. Placed in 1956, the route was one of the first established at the site. The climb is considered a classic, and despite its modest rating remains one of Osman's favorites at the Leap. There are scores of routes at the site, including *Pop Bottle, Preparation H, Pigs on the Wing, Paramour, Bastard Child, Incubus, Epitaph,* and *The Last Sandwich.*

Osman often comes alone to Lovers' Leap and runs laps, free-soloing a number of routes in order as fast as he can climb them (some seven to nine of them for an El Cap day). The routes, from 5.6 to 5.11c, range in height from three to five pitches. Arriving at the top of a route, he runs along the trail through the trees behind the cliff, returning to the base and up the next route without pausing. Sometimes he climbs one route over and over, challenging his fastest time.

To climb *Bear's Reach* from base to summit—three pitches, at 365 feet—a pair of competent climbers will normally require two hours. Much of this time, of course, is spent placing and cleaning protection, resting on ledges, and nibbling on bars of fructose-sweetened horse feed. Free-soloing, Osman's fastest time on the route—nearly leaping, hand over hand—is five minutes and thirty-two seconds, down from his first timed run of 7:16. He will continue to shave seconds off this figure and believes he will eventually climb it in under five minutes.

In the company of Maliska or other climbers, Osman will occasionally "simul-climb" the same routes. Using this technique, two or more climbers will climb simultaneously, without stopping. The leader places protection as he ascends, and the second cleans it, but there are no fixed belays. In alpine climbing, mountaineers commonly simul-climb snowfields and couloirs, placing little if any protection. In such a circumstance, a falling climber's partner or partners *must* belay from their positions, unanchored, and hold his fall. This fails, not infrequently, and a number of the greatest tragedies in the history of mountaineering—including the 1865 catastrophe on the Matterhorn, in which four alpinists were lost for the stumble of a novice—have involved a single climber falling and drawing his fellows after him, yanking them one by one from individually stable but unbelayed positions to their deaths. Likewise, some of the sport's supreme moments have occurred when a single climber, beyond any expectation, holds firm in such a fall and preserves the lives of his entire party. American Pete Schoening saved his six partners on K2 in this fashion in 1953, an event known to mountaineering history as The Belay. In its favor, simul-climbing is fast. At high altitude, speed is safety; the sooner you can get up and off a mountain, the greater your odds of survival. There is a fine line, naturally, between appropriate and reckless speed in the mountains, and accidents all too commonly occur when climbers—through fatigue or inexperience—overstep their technical ability in their desire for haste.

While the route lies well within my ability, I have never climbed *Bear's Reach,* and we will not simul-climb it today. Nor, Osman decides, will he lead it in the classic sense. Instead, he free-solos the first pitch, tailing the rope, and places an anchor at a convenient ledge.

"You're on belay," he calls down.

"Climbing," I shout, chalking my hands.

"Climb on," he calls, and I start up.

As an intermediate climber, bent on improvement, I rarely take the time to climb routes significantly below my technical ceiling. As a result, the activity has become in recent months less a pleasure or a meditation than a vehicle for self-chastisement. I have lost sight, in short, of the reason I took up climbing in the first place. As Alex Lowe phrased it, the best climber in the world is the climber having the most fun. Lowe may well own that title; his technical wizardry aside, his ebullient approach to the steeps is widely known.

On the first pitch of *Bear's Reach*, the holds are abundant, granting me the rare and welcome opportunity of choice. Instead of struggling for the next, tenuous dime edge, I experiment with subtle shifts in balance and move my limbs in steady rhythm. In addition to the vertical crack, there are lie-backs and underclings, pinches and side pulls, crimpers and jugs. For the feet, there is ample friction and the occasional stem. The climbing is a joy.

On a lie-back, I grip a vertical flake, crack, or other formation and "lie back" against it, placing my weight in opposition to my hands. A strenuous technique, this generates a portion of the friction required to remain on the rock. Hand over hand, a climber will often ascend a crack or large flake with a sequence of lie-backs.

An undercling is applied to a downward-pointing rail or flake—a sharp-edged slab of stone that has cleaved partly away from the main face. With one or both hands near the waist, the climber grips the hold and weights it by leaning outward slightly and "lifting" with the muscles of the back and legs. Approached from below, a potential undercling may first surrender to a pinch. The climber may reach up and squeeze the edge of the formation between thumb and fingers, a grip relying entirely on friction and hand strength. Moving the feet up, drawing parallel to the flake, the climber can switch to a two-handed undercling. From there, depending on the route, he or she may reach overhead with one hand to seize a jug—a large, cupped hold also known as a bucket—or a "crimper," a much smaller hold often gripped with the fingers tightly bent, or crimped.

Crimping is hard on the tendons of the fingers; under a sufficient load, fatigued tendons can jump their runners like fan belts, and beginning climbers are encouraged to avoid this grip. With a variation of technique, the same holds can usually be addressed open-handed. As the climber moves past them, the majority of holds change shape in relation to the hand, and the skilled climber has a quiver of grips with which to profit from each position.

A great deal of a climber's expertise comes from his or her ability to read increasingly subtle nuances of rock, of seeing just exactly how—and with what precise amount of weight—to grip a given hold. "There's nothing there" is one complaint heard commonly in bouldering areas, as inexperienced climbers flail on a difficult route. Invariably, there is plenty there. They—and I am all too often among them—simply fail to see it. Like painters who have trained their eyes to differentiate between impossible gradations of grey-blue, the veteran climber will probably see the primary route as plainly as a staircase. Looking closer, such a climber will often discern a number of intriguing alternatives as well, a host of variations upon variations in a face as featureless and slick as polished stone to the impatient newcomer.

On *Bear's Reach*, freed of the perpetual fear of coming off, I consciously examine the hues and textures of the rock. I pause in balance and admire the valley behind me. I've been spending too much time in the gym, I think. Under artificial light, to music, in the confined, competitive atmosphere indoors, it's all too easy to be led astray. On sand-textured plywood and plastic, why waste valuable time on a 5.7? It's not as if you're there for the view.

Perched on the ledge, I clip into the anchor and belay Osman as he runs out the second pitch. To "run it out" is to climb well beyond your last piece of protection—in this case my belay—without placing additional pro. Osman lopes quickly but precisely up the route and sets another three-point anchor at the next ledge. "You're on belay," he shouts again. I clean the anchor at my position, extracting each of the three camming units from a crack and slinging them over my shoulder. "Climbing," I shout back. "Climb on," he responds. Halfway up the second pitch I draw parallel to Osman's acquaintance, anchored and belaying on an adjacent ledge.

"How's it going?" I ask him.

"It takes me a few pitches," he answers, grinning. "Then I feel better."

As I continue up the route, move after move, I settle comfortably into a pace. My attention—broadening and sharpening at once—distills until I respond unconsciously to the demands of the route. My hands and feet move instinctively from hold to hold. I watch the movements of my limbs with some detachment. The fluidity of the climb is coupled with a powerful sensation of groundedness despite my altitude. There is the sense that I am spending not an ounce of strength, that I am drifting skyward, rowing weightlessly across the stone. On this route, on this day, at this easy pace, I decide, I could climb indefinitely. At the top of the route, at the end of the third pitch, Osman greets me with enthusiasm. He taps his watch. Thanks to his full-pitch run-outs, the ascent took forty-eight minutes.

Following the trail to the base of the wall, we rejoin the Warrens and switch partners. While Nikki belays me, top-roped, on the first pitch of *Fantasia*, Cynthia and Osman will attempt to beat our time on *Bear's Reach*. While I climb over-head, Coral, barefoot and unroped, traverses back and forth along the protruding seams—or dikes—of quartz and feldspar at the base of the wall. She is nimble on the rock but overbold, and every few minutes her mother must remind her to remain near the ground.

For much of *Fantasia*, the dikes provide ample holds, and the route would likely be 5.6 without the presence of a modest roof, or horizontal overhang, near the top of the first pitch. In a secondary crux, beyond the roof, the climber must reach across a broad, relatively featureless field of stone for a trio of mushroom-shaped knobs—known as chicken-heads—employed by Royal Robbins in his first ascent of the route in 1973. Robbins may well be the single most important contributor to the develop-ment of American rock climbing, and is commonly revered as such.

Having agreed to meet Osman and Cynthia at the cars, fifteen minutes from the cliffs, Nikki and I break down the gear—three ropes, a heavy rack, and an assortment of slings, shoes, and spare harnesses, and wedge it into two large backpacks, together with spare clothing and the remains of a lunch. Zipping them closed, Nikki hefts both packs—some fifty-odd pounds—and starts down the trail, leaving me with nothing to portage but my day pack. In the debate that follows, I am nearly forced to bar her way to relieve her of one of the packs. This scenario is repeated in miniature some minutes later, when Coral, straining under the weight of her mother's day pack, refuses to surrender it to either of us. We meet Osman and Cynthia at the cars; they have beaten our time on *Bear's Reach* by a minute.

"I time everything," says Osman ironically, securing the packs in his truck, "but I'm always late."

That evening, Osman offers to stamp my climbing hardware with my initials. Earlier in the day, I had admired the identifying marks on his equipment. He produces a boxed set of metal stamps, one for each letter of the alphabet. The stamps stand upright in their slots like bullets, the letters in relief on their tips. Holding each carabiner in place on the broad railing of his deck, he rests the tip of the stamp like a broad, square-sided nail against the carabiner's supported gate and cracks it sharply once with a hammer, imprinting a fine "A" in the aluminum alloy. He repeats this procedure with the second initial, then regards the finished mark like a goldsmith, turning the carabiner in the failing light. Satisfied, he places the piece to the side and reaches for the next.

Many climbers identify their hardware with distinctive

stripes of paint or colored industrial tape. A red and a black band closely set on the spine of a carabiner, for example, or two greens flanking a blue. This can be useful at the conclusion of a long climb—a multiday ascent of El Cap, for example—when two or more climbers' heavy "big wall" racks have cross-pollinated indiscriminately.

. . .

The following day, en route to Maliska's, Osman stops at a South Lake Tahoe gift shop. Cluttered with calendars, potpourris, and the bric-a-brac that thrives like trench foot in tourist destinations, the bookshop-cum-gift boutique bustles with middle-aged women. Dressed in dusty shorts and a climbing jacket, Osman roams the aisles. In such a setting, the climber's poise is all the more apparent for its incongruity. While other customers move vaguely through the labyrinth of aisles, jostling displays, distractedly swiping each other's hips and buttocks with their heavy bags, Osman moves through the crowded confines of the shop with exaggerated, almost paramilitary precision. He yields to other customers at intersections. He slips between revolving racks of nomenclative license plates, herds of ceramic rodents poised on narrow shelves, and ziggurats of snow globes, Lake Tahoe unconvincingly recumbent in their depths.

Osman pauses finally before an assortment of scented candles. After sampling the scents of every variety, he chooses a rose-colored candle the size of a large soup can. An exorbitantly priced bar of soap soon follows, together with a soap tray and a rubber stamp with which a child might imprint her books with

"This Book Belongs To:" in purple ink. While these items are wrapped, Osman carefully ponders the choice of ribbons. Later, in the evening, he will present these gifts to Nikki and Coral for

no particular occasion.

We continue to Maliska's studio apartment in South Lake Tahoe. Kneeling on the carpet in navy-blue climbing shorts and a bleached MTV cap turned backward, Maliska is cutting a fifteen-inch length of black foam tubing with a utility knife to accommodate an autolocking belaying device called a Grigri. Used to fix Maliska's rope to his harness, the Grigri—eight ounces of steel, aluminum, and plastic the size of a taco shell, or in eastern U.S. parlance, a large quahog clam—has been striking him in the face and groin with distressing frequency when he jumps from the top of a tree in his backyard. Maliska is shirtless, his arms and torso leanly muscled. His hair, tucked behind his ears, hangs across his collarbones.

Equipment lies strewn across the floor around him. Within his immediate reach are six coiled ropes of differing diameters and patterns, scraps of black and pale blue foam, a rack of carabiners, and two harnesses. Behind him, over the window, three ice tools jut from the wall as if from vertical ice, their picks buried deep in the Sheetrock. A low table is cluttered with climbing hardware, empty beer bottles, open matchbooks, crumpled and unfinished cigarette packs and laden ashtrays. Despite his evident athleticism, Maliska—like many climbers—has smoked as much as a pack a day for eight years. A climbing headlamp sits atop an ancient television. A motocross helmet lies in a corner. On the top of a high bookshelf, a beige teddy bear peers from behind a kayaking helmet and two pairs of knee and elbow pads. On the shelf beneath, a framed photograph of Maliska's parents stands amidst a collection of rocks, shells, and empty film canisters. Still lower, there are back copies of periodicals: *Climbing, Rock & Ice, Playboy,* and *National Geographic.* There are four Jimi Hendrix records, a plastic bottle of lighter fluid, a collection of naturalist guides, and a modest library including *Black Elk Speaks, World Civilizations,* and *Science and Inventions.*

Topographic maps, science-fiction prints, and autographed climbing posters cover the walls. An electric light Led Zeppelin poster—chromatically alarming, fuzzy to the touch—hangs from the inside of an open closet door.

Above Maliska's bed is a poster of Osman: in the near distance, his back to the camera, he holds himself perpendicular to a near-vertical rock face, a gymnastic pose called a horizontal press. His hands are wide, one above the other. His arms are straight, locked at the elbow. His feet are together, his toes pointed like a diver's. His body, parallel to the earth, is as straight as a pike. He is unroped, far from the ground. I have seen the horizontal press performed on a pole, much nearer to the earth, by the gymnasts of the Canadian-based Cirque du Soleil. Even in that safe, controlled setting, where you expect to be amazed by athletes of the highest caliber, it is a pose that defies belief. Along the right-hand border of the poster is the message "Reality is in fact Virtual." At the bottom it reads,

"Don't let your Fears stand in the way of your Dreams." In the right-hand corner, in stylized flame-red letters, is the name of an outdoor clothing manufacturer: "No Fear." The poster is signed in black Magic Marker: "To Geoff—Thanks for being the friend that you are. 'Pull hard or Die!' Your Bro, Dan O."

In Maliska's bare kitchen, a tie-dyed sheet hangs like a curtain in front of the hot water heater. On top of the refrigerator, empty save for half a deli sandwich and a six-pack of beer, two plastic mugs in the shape of cartoon characters: Wile E. Coyote and the Tasmanian Devil.

Satisfied with the protective qualities of his Grigri guard, Maliska gathers his gear and moves with Osman to the fenced backyard. They spread their equipment out on the decrepit deck. Beside an empty hammock, strung between two pine trees near the deck, two dogs doze while a third gnaws a beleaguered Frisbee. Maliska shares the yard with the occupants of the adjoining apartment. The previous day, while Osman and I ascended *Bear's Reach*, Maliska cleared many months of canine scat and pine needles into an enormous drift along one side of the yard. So exposed, much of the earth beneath is bare of grass. In some quadrants of the yard, the stench of excrement remains potent.

In the far corner of the property, a diving board emerges from the slender tops of a towering two-trunked Jeffrey pine. Eight feet long, ten inches wide, and two inches thick, the board is the side panel of a bed frame, bolted to the tubular crossbeam of a dismantled swing set. Swaying gently in the wind, 95 feet from the ground, the board is the *pièce de résistance* of Maliska's

recently established ropes course. The course includes a 185-f
Tyrolean traverse—a pair of eleven-millimeter static lines
stretched tautly between two pines, declining gently from a
height of 75 to 65 feet.

Maliska lashed the board into position shortly before our
arrival; we will witness his inaugural jump from its prow. Before
its installation, Maliska, Osman, and others leapt in their harnesses from the tree itself. In one instance, Maliska plummeted
some sixty feet, headfirst, and narrowly avoided striking the
swing set, then positioned near the middle of the yard, before
the rope arrested his fall some feet from the earth. Unfazed,
Maliska dragged the offending structure out of range (later dis-
mantling it for parts) and leapt again above the relative safety of
uncluttered ground.

To judge from his behavior, Maliska believes that luck is
inflexible; it is not something you can push. It does not catch up
with you. The chance of disaster is not increased by the frequency of prior successes. In theological terms, the gods do not
expressly punish the bold. "There is no such thing as luck,"
Maliska tells me. "It's all calculated risk."

The simplest model of probability, coin tossing follows a
linear graph. With every throw, the odds of throwing heads is
always 50 percent. Statistically speaking, throwing four heads in
a row in no way reduces the odds of throwing heads again on
your fifth throw. Over time, however, in what is known in probability theory as the law of large numbers, the odds of throwing
nothing but heads become somewhat less than throwing a

roughly proportionate number of heads and tails. In a thousand throws, the ratio of tails to heads should (but may not) grow closer, and still closer in a billion throws. If one were to throw a coin a number of times approaching infinity, one would certainly throw long, unbroken strings of heads—nothing but heads, throw after throw—for many trillions of throws. The same would occur for tails. For other trillions of throws, one would find perfectly alternating results: heads, tails, heads, tails, heads, tails. As well as googols of every other conceivable orderly (apparently) and chaotic (apparently) combination. If you were to come in off the street in the middle of such a series of tosses, to crack the book at random, as it were, and watch 15 million tails thrown in a row, you might begin to suspect that the next throw was going to be tails. You might even place a conservative bet. But the odds would never change. The chance of throwing heads on any given throw would remain, forever and exactly, 1 in 2.

In other games of pure chance—craps, roulette, slots—as in the coin toss, the odds against winning remain constant. In gambling terminology, the commonly held suspicion that fate does indeed catch up with you—for good or for ill—is known as the Monte Carlo fallacy. Casinos do little to disabuse their clients of this visceral assumption, and indeed may subtly reinforce it. Casinos make money because gamblers will continue to bet on long odds after enormous losses largely from the belief—encouraged by free cocktails—that those losses will eventually be counterbalanced by proportionate wins.

All of this is essentially irrelevant to a discussion of tree jumping, or free-soloing, or human life in the main, because none of these are games of pure probability. Physics, not mathematics, plays the greater role here, and physics concerns matter, and matter breaks down. In any case, Maliska's position on this issue—his cool indifference to the Fates, however mysteriously they behave—is one for which I feel both sympathy and admiration. His *modus operandi* may seem foolish, even deranged, in the eyes of one who seeks primarily to prolong life. But in the oldest sense of the term, in the gratuitous, theatrical, self-glorifying tradition of Achilles, it is undeniably heroic. It serves no greater good, and yet inspires.

Maliska dons a purple and hot-pink full-body harness, tightens the straps around his torso and thighs, and clips the Grigri to the load-bearing center of the harness. He moves to the base of the pine and recovers the end of the rope, which hangs from its anchor overhead. He locks the rope into the Grigri, wedges the device into the foam tubing, thumbs the rope into its hollow core, and lashes the guard in place with Velcro straps. So equipped, Maliska ascends the tree. He soon passes the anchor of the Tyrolean traverse, the branches quivering under his weight, and continues to the diving board. Arriving at the altitude of the board, he checks his gear and snaps the slack rope like a whip to clear it of the branches beneath. In a variation of the system developed by Osman on bridges and cliffs, Maliska's rope is anchored dynamically to the Tyrolean traverse lines, twenty feet below. When loaded, the anchor—a pulley backed up by two carabiners—will flex the traverse and the trees that support it. Braked slightly by the carabiners, the pulley will run along one of the cables, toward the center of the traverse, drawing the jumper away from the tree and helping to disperse the forces of the fall. Such is the theory, anyway, and so far the theory has held true.

Maliska steps out onto the diving board, steadying himself with a slender branch in his left hand. Rigidified by the swing set's metal beam, the board flexes only slightly under his weight. Above him, beyond the tapering tips of the pine, the sky is cloudless. A faint gust moves through the upper boughs; Maliska, the board, and the tree sway gently back and forth. Maliska raises his free hand for balance, his eyes on the tip of the board. When the gust passes, he releases the branch and inches out to the tip of the board. He looks down.

"Whoah," he calls. "This is *rad.*"

Osman watches rapt from the ground. A small white patch, illegible from the ground, is stapled to the tip of the board. The patch advertises an athletic shoe manufacturer. Inherited from Osman, who is now backed by a competing manufacturer, the company is Maliska's first sponsor. While good friends, the two climbers have recently had words on this issue. Osman feels that Maliska does not adequately appreciate the help Osman has given him, both as a climber and in establishing sponsorships. He feels that Maliska takes such help largely for granted, and, while talented, is unwilling to devote the months and years normally required to gain professional status as a climber. For his part, Maliska feels that Osman is threatened by Maliska's rapid success and withholds help when it could readily be offered. This rift appears to be symptomatic of Maliska's increasing resentment of his role—in the perception of others—as Osman's sidekick. Some wear the squire's mantle well, indeed prefer it, but Maliska, a charismatic athlete with enormous energy, seems to prefer Batman's cape to Boy Wonder's. More than Osman, who is by nature retiring and self-effacing, Maliska appears to welcome the spotlight.

Maliska doffs his cap and lets it fall to the ground. He gives the rope a gentle shake, confirming its clearance of the branches below. He bounces slightly, flexing the board. He raises his arms in the shape of a cross, takes a breath, and vaults from the board into space.

Maliska pitches out and forward into a rolling, spread-eagled swan dive, plunging seventy vertical feet until the rope runs out of stretch. On impact, the Tyrolean cables shudder, bowing briefly beneath his weight. The pines tremble. There is a whistling, crunching thud as the system is loaded—the crack of hardware being struck together, the singing of the ropes, and Maliska's involuntary, snarling gasp as he slams into the straps of his harness, his limbs snapping loosely to extension. For the fraction of an instant, Maliska hangs motionless in the dead point of his fall. No longer in flight, he is now at his most vulnerable. He is nearest to the ground. The tension on the rope and anchor system is at its greatest. In the case of New Guinea tribesmen, who leap ritually from tree platforms with vines around their ankles, it is the moment when the jumper's forehead should gently brush the ground.

The gear holds. Rebounding, Maliska rockets up and away, across the fence. Spinning on the axis of the rope, he cuts a broad, rising arc across the neighbor's empty, unkempt yard, narrowly missing the branches of another pine, and sweeps back across the fence, over our heads.

"Yeah!" Osman cries. "All right!" As Maliska slows, circling, he unslings the tail of the rope from across his shoulders and lowers it to the ground. Osman seizes the rope and leans back, as if fighting a harnessed horse, and brings Maliska to a halt overhead. Unlocking the Grigri, Maliska rappels down the rope, dropping and braking in a series of short, swift bounces. Above him, the anchor rests near the center of the Tyrolean traverse. Exultant, he touches the ground, unclips from the Grigri, and recovers his hat. Flushed and grinning, Maliska's expression is less one of relief than satiation. He moves to the deck and lights a cigarette.

Osman is soon in position, his toes on the tip of the diving board. From the deck, a portable stereo shudders with heavy metal. The CD is *Roots,* by Sepultura. While the lyrics are indecipherable to my untrained ear, many of the songs, Maliska tells me, are politically environmentalist. Sepultura sounds a good deal more harsh than Metallica, I observe. Maliska nods. "But there's a whole deeper level of heavy metal called grind-core and black metal," he says, watching Osman. "Bands like Mutilated Corpse. They do a song called 'Necrophilia.' They're all pretty sick. A lot of songs about rape and decapitations and torture."

Many of these bands, apparently, hail from Israel or Salt

Lake City. I have never heard these titles in Osman's and Maliska's company, and I gather they do not favor them. Nevertheless, in context, in this barren, dusty yard, in an atmosphere of smoke and excrement, while humans hurl themselves from tree-tops to the sounds of others shrieking, through the twin mouths of the boom box, in formless tones of ire and despair, these casually handled words—rape, mutilation, necrophilia—and the images they evoke, gain a terrifying, almost palpable stature. I feel suddenly agoraphobic, discombobulated, stricken by the perception of a world more vacant and hideous than anything conceived by Bosch: gargantuan eggs with legs like tree trunks, cracked open and spewing cadavers; grinning demons with the beaks of birds sodomizing the souls of the damned. I move to the deck, borrow one of Maliska's cigarettes, and ignite it. The smoke is strong, punishing, cleansing as divine fire. The images of chaos recede. It is only music, after all. It is only dust, and the smell of dogs. Overhead, under an immaculate sky, Osman bounces gently, arms upraised in balance. Maliska watches in amazement. "That looks *so* rad," he says. Undeniably, it does.

Osman performs a pike dive—folding at the waist, touching fingertips to toes—burns his arm on the rope at impact, and clears the neighbor's fence by eleven feet. To establish this figure, I stood still and sighted Osman's path across the fence against the fixed point of a distant pine. While Osman swung to a standstill overhead, Maliska moved to the fence and raised the silver tip of a metal tape measure until it came into line with my sighting. Crude but effective, and the result surprised us all. To the viewer on the ground, at the speed he was moving, it appeared that Osman had little or no room to spare.

Maliska prepares for his second jump. Measuring the slack length with a strip of tape, he feeds an additional five feet of slack through the Grigri. With rope stretch, this should bring him seven or eight feet closer to the ground, and allow him to clear the fence by less than an armspan. Kevin Finnegan, Maliska's neighbor, and Paul Wilson, a mutual friend—both climbers—appear on the deck and follow our attention aloft. While impressed by the visual effect of the board, they have ceased to be surprised by Maliska's antics. They remain on the deck, chatting sociably, and observe the proceedings with near indifference.

Maliska stands backward on the tip of the board, his heels hanging in space. He bounces gently, drops into a squat, and springs back and up into the air. If he feels the slightest hesitation to throw backflips off a diving board ninety-five feet above solid earth—rope or no rope—Maliska fails to betray it. Tucked into a ball, his hands behind his thighs, he performs two and a half revolutions, plunging eighty feet before impacting some fifteen feet from the ground. Compounded by the force of his rotation, the impact is considerably more violent than the first. As Maliska swings to a stop, Kevin shakes his head and disappears inside.

Later, Maliska admits that his apparent fearlessness is "purely cosmetic." "I'm basically a sissy," he continues. "I'm scareder than hell up there." Nevertheless, Maliska believes the system cannot fail. "I have one hundred percent faith in Dan," he says. "I'm not being extreme out here. I'm not going to die."

Before his second jump, in which he intends to throw cartwheels, Osman stands quietly near the middle of the board. He bounces gently, studying the ground. Minutes pass. Unnerved, perhaps, by the rope burn from his previous fall, Osman appears to be stalling. He smiles, then produces a forced, uncomfortable laugh. "This board cracks me up," he calls, shaking his head. Finally, he moves to the end of the board and stands sideways, the outside of his left foot flush with the edge. He breathes deeply, then leaps sideways from the board, throwing two and a half cartwheels before impact.

Maliska lengthens the rope by several feet and throws a last jump for the afternoon—more cartwheels—and impacts thirteen feet from the ground. On the arc of his rebound, he clips branches from the boughs of two pines.

Satisfied, the climbers break down their gear. After three jumps, the straps of Maliska's harness are so tight that he cannot loosen them without Osman's aid. Without reservation, I decline the offer of a jump.

· · ·

I later ask Osman what effect repeatedly putting himself at risk has on his relationships with the people he cares for.

"I feel more blessed to be in their presence," he says. "And I feel more appreciated by them, because they know what I do. They appreciate more fully that I'm alive."

"If you stopped doing all of these dangerous activities," I ask, "do you think the people you care about would care about you any less?"

"I don't think they'd *care* about me less, but I think there would be some loss of respect. I'd lose self-respect, and then others would respect me less. You can't respect someone who doesn't respect himself."

"Your father must be pleased that you're a kind of samurai in the modern idiom."

"Yeah, he is," Osman says, laughing. "And I give credit to my ancestors, to my bloodline. But I think that's my dad's excuse, a way out for what I'm doing. 'He's not just a crazy kid,' he can say. 'It actually comes from samurai blood.'"

"When you were growing up, did your father emphasize the importance of facing your fears?"

"Oh yeah. To face your fears was definitely an unspoken rule."

Osman describes a hunting trip he took with his father at the age of nine or ten. Soon after they arrived at a remote cabin, after dark, they became separated. After calling out several times without response, the younger Osman panicked and began to run, screaming for his father. The elder Osman appeared suddenly from behind a tree and struck him. "The only thing you need to fear out here," he told his son, "is me."

"How would you describe the difference between how you feel when you're with your family and when you're jumping or free-soloing?" I ask.

"Whenever I pull something off—whenever I'm out working, doing what I do—there's a high moment. I feel like I'm on the cutting edge of my own life. The cutting edge. And that's all that really matters. I'm not considering the little things. I'm not summing things up. It's a relief, at that moment, to enjoy the pure physicality of life."

"Conversely, then—with your daughter, for example—do you feel equally present?"

"I feel some guilt, actually. I feel like she should have a hell of a lot more than she has right now. She deserves so much more, and I'm not producing it. So there's definitely a strong sense of inadequacy. It's a real motivator. It makes me really antsy . . . You know, I never realized it, but I get anxiety—anxiety attacks. Are you ever just sitting somewhere, just *rushing* inside? And you're thinking, 'I could be *there*, right now. I could be there doing *that*.' You know? Inside, you're just trapped. So I get anxiety attacks a lot, when I'm in family situations, when I'm spending time with Emma. Even though I totally enjoy it. And it's the time I cherish the most."

"Do you think you could have a satisfying, rewarding life, in which you were financially successful and highly respected for your technical and physical skills, without, in any way, putting your life deliberately at risk?"

He muses over this question for some time. "I don't think so," he says finally.

"So you think putting your life at risk is an essential quality to your life?"

"I think so . . ." He laughs, shakes his head.

"Oh God," he says. "What a fucking realization." Tears

come to his eyes. "You fucker." He continues to laugh. "Oh shit," he says. "It's like admitting something I've never admitted before."

"Do you feel that if you stopped risking your life," I ask, "people would feel that you weren't living your life to the fullest?"

"Yeah. *I* would feel that."

"Do you think it's possible for someone to live their life to the fullest and never knowingly put themselves at great risk?"

"Oh yeah. Absolutely."

"Just not you."

"Just not me . . . And I strongly admire that quality in people, those people who are secure enough in themselves to be able to say, 'You're not getting me out there. I'm fine right here.' "

"You see that as security?"

"Yeah. They're okay to themselves. They don't have to prove anything to themselves. Because that's a big part of what I do. It's proving something to myself. That has everything to do with it."

"What are you trying to prove?"

"That I can step beyond my fears and make logical decisions about what I'm doing."

"Why do you have to do it again and again?"

"An addiction, almost. It's almost an addiction, and there's also the fact that I have to perfect whatever I'm doing. There are still goals I have to attain."

"If you stopped now, would you have proven it to your-self?"

"To myself? Yeah. It's done. It's in the bag. But there's so much more . . ."

"Is there anybody who doesn't believe you? Who questions your courage?"

"Hmmm. Some very influential people in my life, actually."

"Like who?"

"Like my father."

"Your father questions your courage?"

"My courage? Oh. No, no. Maybe I was thinking of the wrong question . . . You kind of lost me there. What was the question?"

"*Who* doubts, somehow, that you haven't really proven it?"

"Oh, okay. It's so complicated, and so easy . . . I don't care. I don't know. Who? I don't know. Do I care? No. It has nothing to do with out there. It's all in here." He touches his temple with a fingertip.

part
three

Mount Shasta rises abruptly from the undulant volcanic plains and forests of California's Siskiyou County to an altitude of 14,162 feet. Like her northern neighbors, Oregon's Mount Hood and Washington's Rainier, Shasta is a dormant volcano, a satellite of the Cascade range. The peak's shaded north side is perpetually girdled with crevassed glaciers and snowfields. On the south side, snow-clad in winter, bare in summer, there are hot springs and trails. Such volcanic peaks, often rising alone from gentle, unlikely landscapes, gain much of their majesty from isolation. Buried in the Himalaya, Shasta would be overlooked as a foothill. *In situ,* observed from a street corner in the adjacent city of Mount Shasta, population 3,500, the mass of the mountain is staggering, out of all scale. Near the summit, snow dazzles between the dark serrated edges of the ridgelines. The observer, gazing from afar, imagines himself there—on that ridge, crossing that brilliant snowfield, clambering up that shadowed gully of hard ice—a minute fleck, ascendant, that shrinks, and shrinks, and finally disappears. While steadily regarding the volcano from a distance, there is a gradual, almost physical sensation of transference, of briefly abandoning one's frail, animated corpse and acquiring instead the mountain's form and logic, its marvelous indifference, its imperturbable aspect of repose.

While a fledgling alpinist, I have been in the proximity of many mountains, from the Alps to the Cascades, and no peak has beckoned to me more, from every angle, than that of Shasta. Only K2, whose severe, classically triangular peak presided over my adolescent bedroom in the form of a poster photograph, exerted an approximately equal pull. Today, when I glance at the folded greeting card of that same Himalayan giant, perched upon my desk between an oblong shard of green stone from a crag in Marin County, and a framed photograph of my wife, seated in the stern of a green wooden dinghy in her bridal gown, I trace the routes upon that mountain that I followed, with my eyes, for years, and I still feel, in a rush, a spasm of desire to ascend, a sudden if transitory willingness to gamble all to stand on the pinnacle of that forbidding pile.

Once called Wyeka, or "Great White," by the Shasta Indians, Shasta continues to be held sacred by many. Indeed, a self-contained New Age subculture has arisen in the vicinity of the mountain. Some of the more conservative among the mountain's worshipers cite the peak as a locus of life force, an alpine Lourdes, an intergalactic signal beacon, a landing pad for extra-terrestrials. I doubt in particular this last claim, if only because the volcanically tortured summit lacks a level surface larger than a standard-sized envelope. "Perhaps," countered a local at the bus station. "But maybe they have very small ships."

At noon on the fourth of August, three weeks after my last visit with Osman, I park with Wayne Greenwell, a climbing partner of long standing, at the end of a maze of deeply rutted logging roads on Shasta's north side. I have known Greenwell since I was a boy; among other forays into wilderness, he spent a number of years married into my immediate family. Greenwell, forty-nine, rock climbs frequently in the Shawangunk Mountains of upstate New York, and in 1994 he spent a month in Nepal, culminating in the ascent of Imja Tse, or "Island Peak," one of a number of so-called trekking peaks in the neighborhood of twenty thousand feet.

Fourteen thousand feet serves as a kind of cutoff in North American alpinism. There are sixty-nine fourteeners, as such peaks are known, in the lower forty-eight United States—fifty-four of them in Colorado—including California's Whitney and Washington's Rainier. Many of these, Shasta and Whitney among them, have actual trails to their summits, accessible on a clear summer day to nearly anyone in good physical shape and a pair of hiking boots. These routes are called walk-ups, dog routes, or escalators by climbers, and while summiting such a peak by way of the trail may be rigorous, it is not considered a climbing ascent. In mountaineering, as in rock climbing, style counts for a great deal.

Mountaineering is distinct from rock climbing in that it involves climbing entire peaks or big walls, often at high altitude, over periods of days, weeks, or even months. Interludes of technical rock and ice climbing notwithstanding, much of a mountaineer's time is spent slogging up ridges, snowfields and glaciers with heavy packs into an increasingly austere, spectacular, and inhospitable environment. The mountaineer must develop a broad, unflagging awareness, often called mountain sense, of subtle shifts in weather, of the varying risk of avalanche, rock fall, and crevasses, and other hazardous and unpredictable aspects of the high ranges.

In Himalayan climbing, the *grande école* of alpinism, the cutoff is eight thousand meters (26,248 feet). There are fourteen "eight-thousanders" in the world, all of them clustered in the Himalayan and Karakorum ranges of Nepal, Tibet, India, Pakistan, and Kashmir. At such an altitude, the oxygen becomes so rare, the weather so capricious, that climbers venturing above it are often fortunate to descend alive. Since May 1953, when Edmund Hillary and Tenzing Norgay made the first successful ascent of Everest, more than 600 climbers have summited the world's highest mountain—8,872 meters, or 29,108 feet.* Over the same period, more than eighty have died in the attempt. (Hillary, a New Zealander on a British expedition led by John Hunt, was knighted by Queen Elizabeth for the accomplishment.) Through 1994 the 8,616-meter,† 28,268-foot K2, the second highest—and statistically most deadly—mountain in the world, had taken 37 lives in trade for 113 ascents. After numerous attempts, K2 was first climbed in 1954 by Italians Achille Compagnoni and Lino Lacedelli, via the Abruzzi ridge. Historically, the odds are formidable.

As in the 1996 Hall and Fischer disaster on Everest, which

---

* This figure, slightly higher than the previously recorded altitude of 8,848 meters, was obtained in a 1987 survey.

† Ibid.

cost five lives, the majority of mountaineering fatalities occur on descent. Storms appear in the mountains with greater frequency in the afternoon, but even under fair skies climbing conditions almost invariably worsen as the day wears on. Under a hot sun, avalanche danger increases with every passing hour, as does the likelihood of popping rudely into a snow-bridged crevasse. Large, open crevasses and vertical faces are often difficult to see from above, and experienced climbers have met their ends by glissading—skiing on their boot soles or backsides—into a crevasse's frigid maw, or off the rail of a thousand-meter face. Few climbers are not fatigued by the time they turn back, from the summit or before. Complicated at altitude by hypoxia, such fatigue should make descending alpinists all the more careful. But many climbers soften their attention in the wake of success. The summiting climber may intuit, incorrectly, that the climb is over, the mountain subdued. The summit may well represent the climax—in the sense of zenith—of the mountaineering experience, but it is no conclusion. This softening tendency is difficult to resist, in part because the climber is tired, and in part because the summit *feels* so conclusive after an arduous ascent. The descent, too often, is considered a mere dénouement. It is a rare climber, and a wise one, who tops out on a difficult peak after hours, days, weeks, or even months of anticipation and often superhuman effort (Himalayan climbers typically lose 15 percent of their body weight on an expedition), and thinks, as he or she attains the long-desired crest: "Halfway." In more rational moments, frequently at gentler altitudes, every reasonable climber tries. "The climb begins and ends at base camp," they intone.

"You're on the mountain until you're off the mountain." But the tendency remains.

A few words on oxygen and atmospheric pressure: Regardless of altitude, the air around us is composed of nitrogen (nearly 80 percent) and oxygen (more than 20 percent), as well as traces of other gases. The so-called partial pressures of these gases, and the rate at which they are absorbed into the body, lower as the altitude rises. Under atmospheric pressures greater than that of sea level, this operates in reverse: for a scuba diver approaching depths of three hundred feet, the mass of oxygen absorbed into the bloodstream is so great that the life-preserving gas becomes toxic, and will prompt convulsions. Likewise, the absorption of nitrogen increases at depth, producing its own, infamously narcotic effect. Known poetically as the "rapture of the deep," faint nitrogen narcosis feels nearly identical to the effect of nitrous oxide, or laughing gas, administered by dentists. Like alcohol, excessive nitrogen in the blood results in disorientation, euphoria, and impaired judgment, and "narced" divers have been killed by simple mistakes made under its influence. Like variations in alcohol tolerance, divers respond differently to different depths: some become giddy at sixty feet; a rare few remain sober at two hundred. To compensate for these and other dangers associated with gas absorption, divers working at extreme depths manipulate the ratios of gases in their tanks, reducing the amount of nitrogen and oxygen through the addition of harmless, inert gases, such as helium.

The climber at altitude faces an inverse danger. A quart of air bottled at the summit of Mount Whitney is lighter, and less nourishing, than a quart drawn in Death Valley. The problem is a function not of volume, but of mass. For every foot you climb above sea level, there are fewer molecules of oxygen in every inhaled breath. At eight thousand meters, there are approximately two-thirds less. The Himalayan climber, in effect, is gradually suffocated, even while gasping for air.

Austria's Reinhold Messner, widely considered the greatest mountaineer of all time, was the first to ascend all fourteen of the world's peaks in excess of eight thousand meters. In 1978 Messner and partner Peter Habler ascended Everest without supplementary oxygen, when medical experts assured them it could not be done—that even the attempt would likely kill them. The same year, Messner was the first to solo an eight-thousand-meter peak: Nanga Parbat. Two years later Messner returned to Everest and soloed the more challenging north face, again without oxygen. During a talk and slide show in Berkeley several years ago, Messner described the anguishing loss of his younger brother Günther in an avalanche in 1970, on a descent from Nanga Parbat. He recalled falling into a crevasse at night while climbing alone, high on another Himalayan peak. It took him hours to find a way out of the crevasse—a deep, frozen slit in the hide of an enormous glacier. At one point, Messner claimed, he swore to God that if he made it out alive he would immediately descend and never climb again. When he finally did emerge into the moonlight, he confessed to the audience in an accent very like Arnold Schwarzenegger's, "something told me to go up." Discarding his oath, Messner continued to the summit in short order. Despite this and other, similar accounts of boldness bordering on reckless disregard, other prominent mountaineers are quick to praise Messner for his willingness to back down in poor conditions, and largely attribute his enduring survival to this trait.

Many rock climbers are left cold by mountaineering; some of the finest have never put their hand to an ice axe. Correspondingly, some dedicated mountaineers view technical rock climbing as little more than a means to an end, gaining only enough proficiency on rock to ascend the great peaks. To be sure, there are superb generalists, equally content and skilled on overhanging rock, frozen waterfalls, and Himalayan faces.

In mountaineering, then, one might imagine that the mountain is the measure of the climber. But every mountain is a hundred or a thousand mountains, depending upon variations of style, route, and weather. Compared to soloing, climbing the same peak in a guided expedition is entirely a different game. The snowless south side of a mountain encountered by a day hiker on a cloudless summer afternoon can resemble the glaciated north side of the same peak, in an early autumn storm, to the degree that a motel swimming pool in Las Vegas resembles the North Sea in a gale.

Greenwell and I plan to ascend Shasta via the right side of the Hotlum glacier, a route of moderate difficulty on the peak's north side. For my part, I realize, the ascent will serve as a form of prepartum preparatory exercise. My wife's pregnancy has been uneventful, even pleasant; partly for this reason, and partly out of fear of the alternative, I anticipate a fairly smooth delivery. The labor, I augur unwisely, will span no more than eight to ten

hours. While pleased by my optimism, Erin makes no such pre-
dictions, and we remain diligent in our daily exercises. If the
Fates do choose to smile upon us, we will certainly meet them
halfway. My guesswork aside, I still harbor considerable fear of
the actual birth. I have never witnessed childbirth and wonder if
I have the stomach for it. I have heard the tales of men passing
out and getting sick, of men requiring more assistance—moral
and in certain cases medical—than their wives.

In short, while I am titularly current in first aid and CPR
from the American Red Cross, and may remember, *in extremis,*
that the ratio of compressions to breaths in one rescuer CPR is
15 to 2 and not the other way around, I am not as comfortable
with medical procedures, with ambient blood, as I would like
to be.

In any case, with the approach of the delivery, and a corre-
sponding rise in anxiety, I have felt increasingly compelled to
climb a substantial peak. On the one hand, I know the climb is
motivated by my thrashing, adolescent terror at the prospect of
approaching responsibility. Thrilled on the one hand by the
prospect of fatherhood, I often catch myself, in undistracted
moments, in a panic. The climb, then, will serve as a distraction,
a reprieve. High on Shasta, my worries will be concrete but few.
And while I do not count myself among those expectant fathers
who envy their wives the explicit experience of childbirth, I suspect that the ascent of Shasta will serve as a kind of surrogate, if
far inferior, challenge.

Four years ago I made an attempt on the north side of
Shasta with Erin, her brother Jeff Davis, and his Swedish fian-

cée, AnnaStina Hoeglin. From a rocky camp at 9,500 feet we made our first bid for the summit under clear skies. All went well until, lunching on English cucumber, Monterey Jack, sardines and crackers, benched upon our packs in a stone-walled crow's nest near 11,000 feet, the women decided that they lacked the necessary experience for the route. We aborted the climb and retreated, deciding that Jeff and I would make another bid for the summit the following morning, leaving the others safely in camp. At daybreak, a gloom appeared across the plains to the northwest. "It'll blow over," we decided, incorrectly, and set off. The sky continued to darken as we ascended the first snowfield, trudging unroped in the direction of the Hotlum glacier. The air was motionless. Our boots crunched rhythmically through the frozen crust. At the top of the snowfield we paused for breath. We glanced back, into the gathering blackness to the north. At that precise moment, as if to preempt our reconsideration, we were blasted by a seventy-mile-per-hour wind.

On the heels of the wind came sleet and lightning. As we sprinted down the snowfield, back to camp, the bolts struck the ridges on either side, above and beneath us—some as close as a hundred yards—with magnificent reports. We leapt across the stones at the base of the snowfield and came into view of our camp. Erin sat curled in a ball. Stina ran to and fro, crouching, recovering small items of gear. Jeff's tent yawed and buckled under the wind, but my own was nowhere to be seen. The wind, we soon discovered, had struck the tent while Erin was stepping through the door, ripping out the stakes and throwing her heavily to the ground, stunning her and bloodying her wrist. Loaded with our packs and sleeping bags, the three-man dome sailed up and away and down the mountain out of sight.

Waiting out the weather was unthinkable; we had to lose altitude and get under the storm, out of the lightning and the freezing rain. With Erin partially revived, the two women tore down the surviving tent, stuffed it directly into a pack, and hurried, crouching, down the trail. Jeff and I bound down the sloping boulder field in search of the lost shelter. We found the tent, unbelievably, a wad of blue and grey between two stones. The fly and the floor were torn to ribbons, the fiberglass poles splintered in their sheaths. But the packs were there, within, together with the sleeping bags, now sodden. Wadding all of it together, we traversed to the trail and our companions. Descending swiftly, we soon emerged, as if passing through a trapdoor, into arid sunlight and stillness. We paused to collect ourselves. While the storm played on the heights above—the peak concealed above an impenetrable lid of black, flickering sky—lizards basked on the rocks at 9,000 feet. Rested, we hiked to the roadhead and laid out our gear, in the dusty heat, to dry. All told, we were lucky.

Now, Greenwell and I leave the same trailhead at one o'clock. Traveling at an easy pace, we arrive at the same camp—near 9,500 feet—at six. The next morning we move to a higher camp near 10,000 feet, amidst the stones near the foot of the glacier. The forecast for the week is favorable, and at eleven o'clock the sky is cloudless to the far horizon. After lunch we spend several hours practicing crevasse rescue. A wind works the summit overhead, stirring up huge spindrifts of snow along the ridgeline to the east. The formations spiral and distort into dragons with yawning jaws and taloned forelegs. Two climbers appear minutely, far above, descending the Hotlum glacier. We watch them, through binoculars, as they approach the long grey slash of a huge, open crevasse. They pause above it, reconsider, and make a long traverse around to the west.

Roped together, hiking on the glacier, Greenwell and I take turns performing mock crevasse falls. The possibility of dropping into an actual crevasse is exceedingly remote, given our intended route. To discount its possibility entirely, however, would be a grave mistake, as it would on any glaciated peak. For one thing, the weather may change. One mountaineer of my acquaintance, far more experienced than I, has made five or six attempts on the mountain over the years, each time repelled from the summit by violent storms. High on the mountain, Greenwell and I could find ourselves in a whiteout—a driving snowstorm that renders the terrain invisible. Descending in such conditions, the leader could easily wander off route, straight into a frozen hole. If we are fortunate and careful, these skills may never be used. Yet they remain, perhaps, the most important skills we have, and it behooves us to practice them under a clear sky.

As we move across the glacier, with or without warning, one of us lunges violently against the rope to simulate a fall. The rescuer—jerked from his feet—must first arrest the fall with ice axe and boots. From this braced position, he must place an anchor in the snow and divert the victim's weight from his harness to the anchor. We are each equipped with snowflukes, aluminum wedges that, when buried at the correct angle, serve as anchors.

Freed of the victim's weight, the rescuer must rapidly construct a pulley system with carabiners or lightweight pulleys and extract the "unconscious" victim from the "crevasse." The victim, in these drills, leans back in his harness uncooperatively, forcing the rescuer to winch him up the slope. This is more challenging than it sounds, and we work up a sweat before retiring for an early dinner. Ominously, Greenwell appears to have strained a muscle in his upper back during the course of these exercises; in an effort to simulate the shock of actual falls, we may have been overzealous. Under an immaculate dusk, we review the route, prepare our equipment, and retire to our sleeping bags at nine. Greenwell sets his watch alarm for 2:00 the following morning.

· · ·

As a youth, I flirted with the idea of joining the Marine Corps as an exercise in physical courage. Historically, the marines are known for their ability to sustain heavy casualties in pursuit of their objectives. They take pride in the fact that they will die sooner than leave their wounded behind; indeed, hundreds of marines have been killed in attempts to recover wounded comrades from exposed positions under heavy fire. Upon the mind of a boy preoccupied with daring, this kind of mythology can work a considerable spell.

I never did enlist. I worked for a year following high school, spent six months traveling overseas, and came home to a college education at Berkeley. Politically, I am no militant—it is the response of individuals to challenging environments that intrigues me—but when I expressed, offhandedly, my interest in the Marine Corps to a group of peers at Cal, they regarded me with uniform expressions of betrayal.

I knew I'd never fit into the Corps; I had far too severe an authority problem. To such an individual, the *idea* of the marines may well be alluring. But the realities of enlisted armed service would be something else entirely. Boot camp would be fine, I thought, as long as some idiot—a drill instructor, for example—didn't try to tell me what to do. I'd be out on my idealistic ass, in short, furious and disillusioned, before the ink dried on my enlistment papers.

In 1945 my father was an eighteen-year-old radar operator aboard an American aircraft carrier in the Pacific. He himself had attempted to join the marines but was refused on the basis of slight nearsightedness. Ten years later, as a foreign correspondent based in Paris with a wife and three children, he reported the 1955 Massacre of Oued Zem in Morocco. The following year, he crossed the Hungarian border, illegally, to cover the Hungarian Revolution. On the day after Soviet tanks rolled out of Budapest, feigning defeat, as the Hungarians rejoiced in the boulevards, hauling the statues of Lenin and Stalin from their pedestals, the Nationalists began to exact their revenge on the remnants of the Communist Secret Police. Groups of disarmed prisoners were corralled into rooms and gunned down. Others were beaten senseless in the streets and shot dead. Their bodies were stripped, taunted, kicked, and spat upon by soldiers and civilian bystanders.

Late in the afternoon, in the company of *Life* photographer John Sadovy, my father approached a Hungarian tank crouched at the edge of a grassy park near the city center. Driven by defected Hungarian soldiers, the tank roared suddenly to life and rolled in the direction of a broad stone building across the park, the headquarters of the secret police. Joining a throng of armed men, the two journalists trotted after the machine. As the tank appeared in the open, the square erupted with the sound of concentrated gunfire—automatic small arms, for the most part, directed at the tank by the secret police from the windows and steps of the building. The air immediately began to buzz with passing rounds. Leaves and branches were clipped from surrounding trees. My father continued to run in a half-crouch, blindly, following the tank. He was hit almost immediately in the left hand, then pulled down out of fire by a Hungarian running beside him. The bullet had passed through the second knuckle of his third finger and embedded itself in his palm. (Sadovy ducked behind a tree, unharmed.) Retreating after the firing subsided—overwhelmed, the secret police finally surrendered—my father was treated in a Budapest hospital crowded with wounded Hungarians before returning to Paris.

During my childhood, my father—commuting by train to an editor's desk in New York City—rarely spoke of these experiences. But as a boy of six or seven I often stared at the bent knuckle on the ring finger of his left hand, and asked myself if I, too, would have the good fortune to be shot. I had no interest whatever in being killed. From the same age, I wanted no less to be a father, to live long.

During the early months of Erin's pregnancy, my father visited alone from the East. As he and I returned from a neighborhood walk, pausing in the driveway, I asked him if he thought it important for a writer to see combat. I suppose I expected him to say no. Perhaps, on some level, I hoped his answer would exempt me. He might have said, "Only if the writer lacks imagination." While he encouraged his children to be athletic and self-reliant, he never urged us to take physical risks. Despite his explosive, intermittent anger, there was never any talk, in the classic sense, of acting like a man. But as we stood in my driveway, he surprised me. He answered mildly but without hesitation: yes, he believed it was. He appeared sorry I had asked. That was all, and we went inside for lunch.

. . .

Greenwell and I doze fitfully on Shasta, from anticipation and the effects of altitude, but manage to sleep through the alarm. I wake suddenly at three-thirty. While the moon lies concealed behind the mountain, the sky is clear, the glacier luminous with starlight. A breath of wind moves across the glacier from the west. After breakfast and minor equipment delays we leave camp shortly after five.

We wear helmets—primarily for rock fall—and crampons. In summit packs we carry lunch, water, cameras, additional warm layers of clothing, and first-aid kits. In our uphill hands, passed back and forth as we cut switchbacks up the glacier, we carry ice axes. The axe aids in balance and will be used, in case of a fall, for self-arrest. In the bright starlight, we have no need of our headlamps. We are roped together with fifty feet of line between us, the remainder coiled in equal halves across our shoulders. Clipped to our harnesses, out of the way but within easy reach, are snowflukes, pulleys, and spare carabiners.

I lead, with Greenwell following at such a distance that the rope is neither taut nor slack, but swings between us, brushing the snow. We call back and forth, calibrating our pace. The surface of the glacier, pocked like a wind-ruffled bay, is glazed at this hour with a thin crust of ice. Eschewing the rocky Hotlum-Bolam ridge to the west, we strike a straight line for the summit, ascending the Hotlum glacier toward a broad rock field checked with snow. The lower reaches of the glacier are not steep, but on the slick surface an unarrested fall would gain potentially deadly momentum, delivering us like skipping stones to the rocks at the glacier's foot. To a climber, even the gentle, thirty-degree slope near the glacier's base feels intuitively closer to forty-five. Shasta may not lie in the Himalaya, but like any substantial, glaciated peak it commands respect. More than forty climbers have been killed upon its flanks, usually as the result of storms and simple errors.

With the understanding that numeric ratings are insufficient and often misleading in mountaineering, where so many factors, on any given day and route, must be considered, I asked Andy Selters to put Shasta into some kind of global perspective. Selters, an expert mountaineer and guide based in California, wrote the definitive guide on the mountain—*The Mount Shasta Book*—with Mike Zanger. At first, citing the reasons outlined above, Selters was hesitant to hazard any numeric comparisons. "On a scale of world mountaineering from, say, one to fifty," he said finally, "with the most difficult faces in the Himalaya pushing fifty, Shasta's south side might rank in the single digits, and her north side in the ten-to-fifteen range." Shasta, he agreed, might be compared to some of the moderate peaks in the French Alps. "No one climbing Shasta is going to think they're breaking any new ground," he continued, "but it's a big mountain, and the weather is unpredictable. A friend of mine was stranded in a storm, low on the Hotlum glacier, and one of his partners was killed. There is an increasing tendency to judge peaks by technical difficulty alone, and this is dangerous."

Out of religious respect, the Shasta Indians did not climb the peak. A white man, E. D. Pearce, made the first confirmed ascent in 1854.

The sun tops the horizon before six, a flaming tangerine reflected on the glacier's frozen plate. We soon attain the rock field, drawing level with the long crevasse to the east. While picking our way between rock piles, I try to subtly maximize our gain of altitude with every step. This is not unlike the attitude of the helmsman, in sailboat racing, while beating toward a windward mark. The sailor schemes and wheedles constantly on every tack, shaving the angles—not too far, of course, for then he'll pinch the wind and lose speed—until he makes the mark. A climber tacks, in this sense, up the mountain, cutting switchbacks, where necessary, to conserve strength. Up, up, up, you think, like a mantra, and cheat your way up the peak. You shave five degrees off a switchback. You steepen your route to leave the approaching rock pile downhill. Whenever possible, you abandon switchbacks and toe-kick up the slope in a direct line. Without altering the rhythm of your steps, you increase the length of your stride by an inch or two. Your partner, following in your tracks, may not even notice the change, but over the course of a thousand steps, you will gain an extra pitch. And while you cannot always see the summit, you know—from prior examination from afar, from the topographical map, from glimpses on the route—where it lies. You do not rush, but your desire for the summit grows with every step.

By midmorning, the sun hammers the mountain. Where struck by the ascendant sun, the snow softens. In the shadows, within the gullies and behind rock outcroppings, it remains crusty, spotted in places with hard ice. We have stripped to our Capilene shirtsleeves, donned glacier goggles, and coated our cheeks, noses, and lips with zinc oxide, greasy white. At these heights, doubled in reflection from the snow, the sun is merciless. As additional protection I have fashioned, on a previous climb, a nose guard from a wedge of moleskin, or blister padding. In preparation for a day on a glacier, I once made the mistake of forgetting to protect my lower lip with sunscreen. It is not an error one is likely to repeat. An afternoon was adequate to sear the lip with a second-degree burn. In the following days it swelled to twice its ordinary volume, blistered over, and took two miserable weeks to heal. When I was sixteen, during a month-long course with the National Outdoor Leadership School in Wyoming's Wind River Range, I neglected my glacier goggles for an hour or two on a snowfield. For this oversight I was given a taste of snow blindness—when the skin of the eyeball is sunburned. That night in the tent, my eyes itched terribly. The discomfort subsided by morning, but in severe cases the sensation is reportedly agonizing—victims cannot see for hours or days, and compare the sensation to having fine sand rubbed against the surface of the eyeballs.

As the morning wears on, gaining altitude, Greenwell's upper back begins to tell. We take frequent rests, allowing him to shed his pack and stretch. Nearing thirteen thousand feet, he is in enough pain to threaten the climb. "You may have to do it without me," he says, during a rest. I am already nauseated from the altitude, and my head—above the eyes, behind the temples—pounds steadily. I feel slightly dazed by the diminishing oxygen, and while not consciously winded, I try to compensate with slow, deep breaths. These symptoms, at least, are not as severe for Greenwell, who has been taking prescription medication—the surplus from his Himalayan trip—to help acclimatize. The drug, Diamox, expands the blood vessels, allowing a more rapid transfer of available oxygen. I refused the drug, curious to discover how I would respond to fourteen thousand feet without acclimatization.

I am unwilling to leave him, of course; we will abort the climb if necessary. But I'm loath to turn back while he is still able—even at a crawl—to continue. Shasta has nagged at me steadily for the last four years, and the summit feels too close to abandon.

"You'll make it," I tell him. There is a fine line between encouragement and coercion, but I tell myself, perhaps selfishly, that Greenwell knows his limits. We set off again, up another steep snowfield toward a pair of prominent rock spires. I lead at a creep, breathing, counting every step from one to eight. At every count of eight I pause, lower my head to my chest, and relax completely, resting the heel of my palm on the head of the ice axe. I close my eyes and sink deep into my stance, one foot higher than the other. I take several long breaths before I open my eyes and begin again; one—two—three—four.

Despite the pain, or perhaps in part because of it, the climbing is profoundly meditative and satisfying. My mind—ordinarily a punted hornet's nest of anxieties, desires, and ambitions—is pleasantly sedated by the hypoxia, its functions at once disabled and focused by the headache and the rhythmic simplicity of the climbing itself. The incessant, conflicting voices of the mind are quiet, and in their place, between the slow, piercing beats of the ache, is nothing but a cooling hiss, the sound of a light rain on a tent fly.

Greenwell follows for a time and then collapses. I quickly drop to his position, help him from his pack. The pain in his back is excruciating, and for a moment I accept that the climb is over. I watch my partner, suffering in the snow, and feel a sharp, sudden anger—at the mountain, at Greenwell—for denying me the summit a second time. "Give me your weight," I tell him. In too much pain to argue, Greenwell lets me empty most of the contents of his pack into my own. I quickly reconfigure the rope, tying Greenwell into the tail, feeding out fifty feet between us and coiling the remainder over my shoulder. While the weight itself is negligible, the effect on Greenwell is transformative. He rises grimly to his feet and turns for the summit. I move back up the slope, taking up the slack, and we climb on.

We pass the two spires and ascend a short, steep gully of

mixed snow, rock, and ice. As I near the top of the gully I am struck by the environment's austerity. Apart from the crunch and tink of our crampons and tools, there is no sound, no movement. I pause to listen, breathing. Above me, the sun strikes the ice of the gully in an unflickering white flash. Briefly, the headache seems to pass. The nausea softens. I stare at the melting surface of the ice. I glance up the barrel of the gully, into the empty sky. There is absolutely nothing here, I think. "It's beautiful," I holler down to Greenwell, and laugh suddenly out loud. Later, I learn that a number of climbers have been killed in falls from this gully.

When I top out of the notch the sickness returns and worsens. I have never had a headache this severe and I'm very close to throwing up. How much farther, I think morosely, can it be? We continue left, around another outcropping onto a snowfield. In the shade of the outcropping I sag into the snow to rest; I lower my head and crush my temples with the heels of my palms. The view is spectacular—hundreds of miles of Californian and Oregonian semiwilderness, a conical peak rising snowcapped in the center of the northern horizon—but in my condition it does not register. I am almost unaware of Greenwell, resting silently near me. Oddly, perhaps, my desire for the summit does not diminish as the pain increases. In fact, the higher we get—the more my body sickens, the more myopic, surreal, and withdrawn my perspective—the more I want to ascend. I can perceive only one escape: to go up.

Altitude sickness takes various forms, and in mountaineering lore there are accounts of rational climbers becoming unstable, even belligerent, from the effects of oxygen starvation. In one such incident, a climber in the Alps became irate and attempted to attack his two companions. By good fortune, he was positioned in the middle of the rope, and incapable, in his delirium, of untying. His partners leaned back in their positions, pinning him in his position on the slope. Lunging in his harness, bellowing obscenities, the ordinarily mild alpinist threatened his partners with his ice axe until he finally collapsed, stuporous with exhaustion. His rope mates quickly lowered him to a more hospitable altitude, and when recovered he could not recall the event. I would not suspect myself of mayhem—such a reaction is exceedingly rare, if not unique—but if Greenwell quit, I later reflect, might I have untied from the rope, abandoned him, and staggered up the final heights alone?

I finally take four aspirin from my first-aid kit and rise to my feet. Wordlessly, we continue on. We have barely started up the next snowfield before I suspect that the summit lies atop its crest. Beyond the shoulder of the snowfield, bracketed by contortions of volcanic rock, there is nothing but sky. This is also true in the case of false ridges—where one excitedly tops a rise only to discover, beyond, another ridge—but we are very high. There simply cannot be much more mountain to ascend. "That's it," I call back to Greenwell. A last, colossal surge of adrenaline electrifies my limbs. Drawing the rope taut, I churn in a direct line up the slope. If I were not tied, I would run. Greenwell himself is renewed—I do not look back but I can feel, through my harness, a fresh liveliness at the end of the rope. He is following fast.

That evening—having summited before noon, glissaded back to camp in two and a half hours, and staggered out to the roadhead—Greenwell raises a beer in a dim Mexican restaurant in Mount Shasta city.

"Two up, two down," he says. And we drink.

. . .

Late on the fourth of October, two weeks before her due date, Erin goes into labor. While we have our list—with everything from a tennis ball to help counter the pain of back-labor to a receiving blanket—we have yet to pack for the hospital. The cradle is ready, standing empty on Erin's side of the bed. The changing table is in place. We have finished our childbirth classes. Erin is prepared. But I am not ready. Good Christ, I think. I'm not ready.

Shortly after two the following morning—both of us anxious and unable to sleep—Erin has her first real contractions. While the uterus prepares for labor, in the final weeks, with isolated "Braxton Hicks" contractions, these are more intense and arrive in intervals under ten minutes. We're in it now—all three of us—and there is only one way through.

By morning, neither of us has slept a wink. At the doctor's advice, we attempt to doze for a couple of hours at midday. I drift in and out of consciousness, but the contractions prevent Erin from sleeping. As the afternoon wears on, the contractions intensify. By eight in the evening, Erin can no longer walk through them.

At nine o'clock, as the doctor advised, we drive to the

hospital. I quickly pack the trunk and help Erin down the steps to the garage. It is dark; the avenues are mysteriously empty.

At the hospital Erin is checked into the maternity wing and is soon moved into a delivery room. With warm walls and curtains and a rose ceramic lamp on the nightstand, the room is comfortable, even homey, despite the requisite black terminals, dial-studded and bristling with hoses. Another nurse appears, calm and maternal, followed by Erin's labor coach, or doula, who will be with us throughout the labor and delivery.

The doula never leaves Erin's side. She suggests new positions for the contractions—in the chair, leaning against the bed, in the bathroom. She proposes a hot shower, and Erin and I walk down the corridor to the shower room, pausing and leaning through the contractions. The nurse places a plastic chair in the shower, drapes it with a towel, and Erin sits, exhausted, in the streaming hot water. I kneel and sit beside her, out of the shower, in the steam. She is starting to feel trapped by the labor. She hasn't slept in thirty-six hours. "I don't want to go through with this," she says. "I'm scared."

As the night wears on, things get worse, and then much worse, but Erin refuses painkillers. She fears that drugs will make it worse, that they will slow her down, distract her, disrupt her ability to focus. The pain may be more severe without them, she argues, but at least she will know—to the degree our senses tell the truth—what is going on. Her doctor appears, in the early hours of morning, and breaks her waters to hasten the labor. So it does, but the baby's head, descendant, traps the lip of Erin's cervix against her pelvic bone. In such cases, when the baby drops before the cervix has completely dilated, the cervix, disastrously, may tear. "You can't push," commands the nurse. "You cannot push."

Erin groans and writhes as if branded during the following contractions, fighting the urge to push for more than half an hour. Between contractions, the nurse finally manages to coax the cervix up and out of the way with a gloved fingertip. Erin begins to push, but she and her uterus—twenty-nine hours into her labor—are exhausted. With each contraction she pushes, until the baby's head finally crowns, a slick lozenge of skin, dark with hair, rolling briefly into view before slipping back and out of sight. The doctor soon appears and affixes a wire, minutely hooked, to the baby's scalp. The wire, inflicting a nearly invisible wound, is connected to a fetal monitor, which precisely measures the infant's heart rate. For some reason, the baby is delayed in the constrictive narrows of the birth canal. While traversing the canal, the umbilical cord is often pinched, limiting the amount of oxygen available to the infant. Indeed, this now appears to be the case; as the monitor reveals, the baby's heart rate is dangerously low and dropping.

Erin is immediately put on oxygen, to strengthen her and flush her bloodstream—and the baby's—with the precious gas. She continues to push. With the doula on her left side, I stand on Erin's right. I hold her head in one hand, her knee in the other. The strain of pushing has burst scores of blood vessels in her face—around the translucent green oxygen mask, her mottled cheeks and brow are freckled with purple specks. The oxygen stabilizes the baby's heart rate, but there is precious little time to lose. The baby's head finally emerges. Facedown, the baby's head is oblong, purple-grey, the size of a grapefruit. The pale, blue-veined umbilical cord is wrapped tightly twice around its neck; this constriction was the cause of the delay. With his forefinger, the doctor unhooks the cord and coaxes out an arm. In a rush, the remainder of the baby slips clear, into his hands. It is 8:18 on Sunday morning, October 6.

"It's a girl," the doctor says, and my heart leaps. Blue and quivering, she could fit in my two hands, and the doctor places her carefully on Erin's chest. The nurses cover them both with warmed blankets. Erin holds the baby, and begins to weep. I gaze in shock at the pair. I had been warned, by popular accounts, that newborn human infants—bloody and misshapen— are alien and unattractive at birth, even to their parents. Perhaps this child is an exception, I think; perhaps my judgment is impaired by fatigue. But she is the most beautiful living thing that I have ever seen.

Minutes later Erin begins to bleed. Her uterus, exhausted by the labor, is not closing down as it must to stop the arterial bleeding caused by the placenta's separation from the uterine wall. "We're losing a lot of blood here," the doctor calls to his nurses, alarmed. I stand as if coldcocked.

A nurse lunges past me, striking the emergency button; others dash from the room. The doctor calls for petocin, a naturally occurring hormone that stimulates the uterus to action. A nurse jams a hypo of the drug into Erin's thigh. They prepare for a transfusion. "This is going to hurt," says the doctor, and thrusts his hand entirely into Erin's uterus. She cries out in pain. He sweeps his fingertips across the bleeding wall, tearing off the clots to stimulate closure. When he withdraws his hand, more blood pours into a steel pan. She has lost a quart of blood in three minutes. He kneads the uterus through the skin of her abdomen, pressing it down. Miraculously, the bleeding slows and halts before they have to administer the transfusion. I am faint, and sit heavily on a footstool. I lower my head to my knees.

After the baby is weighed, measured, and checked, the three of us are left alone. The carts and trays and pans are wheeled from the room. Erin holds the baby, in a swaddle and knit cap. The baby's face is bright red and exotic. Her eyes, opening intermittently in slits, are a deep iron blue, whiteless, like the eyes of some strange and ancient reptile.

After a time, as Erin gazes at the baby, I pace the empty room and attempt to regather my wits. In the sun, Erin's blood lies spotted and dry on the tiles near the foot of the bed. There are only five or six errant drops, the diameter of quarters, uncaught by towels and pans. I take a damp paper towel from the bathroom and bend down, wringing the water from the towel onto the tiles. I wipe up the blood and inspect it. The sweet, pungent smell of the reconstituted blood unsettles and alerts the mind. It is the smell of Erin's life. I clean the floor deliberately, completely, as if licking a wound.

The following morning I wake at dawn in the recovery room. Erin sleeps beside me, on her side. The baby, whom we have named Julia, sleeps in the bassinet beside the bed. The wing of the hospital is completely silent. Throughout the night, nurses have come in and out of the room, checking them both. I wake into a feeling of such love for the child that I can scarcely breathe. I am refreshed, after a sleep, and the shock of the event has dissipated; my emotions run clear. As I lie there, I am catapulted back into the labor. Stunned by the scale of the events, increasingly fatigued, I experienced the actual labor as a dream. Now, however, I am perfectly awake, and as I recall the baby's flattening heart rate, I begin to hyperventilate. In a moment my body is trembling uncontrollably. The room itself is shaking, crumbling around me with a roar. I am unable to break myself from the experience. The baby is not getting air. I cannot get control of my breathing. The panic descends so quickly that I cannot begin to control it, as I had in the Pacific cave.

In the high ranges there are avalanches that are so incalculably massive, and move so fast, driving a wall of air before them, that climbers in their path are blasted from the face by the wind before the snow ever reaches them. I have never been hit by an avalanche, but in the hospital bed I am struck so fast and hard by such a fear that it feels as if I am going to disintegrate, to rip apart. I clutch the sheet with my hands. Erin is bleeding and I can't stop it. The blood is running from her. I am drowning. The ceiling is upon my chest and crushing me. My bones are snapping. I am choking, gasping for air.

I throw myself suddenly to the floor, kneel on the tiles, and lean into the seat of the chair. I crush my hands together and grind my forehead, brutally, against my clasped hands. I cannot escape. My wife and child are dying and I cannot help.

The walls stop shaking, suddenly. The roaring is extinguished.

There is someone else in the room. I can feel the distinct presence of Erin and Julia, alive behind me, as clearly as I can feel my two hands, clasped the one within the other. But there is another, near the foot of the bed behind me, closer to the ceiling than the floor. I do not look. I know exactly where he is. I know that he has taken not a neutral nor a female but a male form, and in context this surprises me. With the knowledge of his presence comes the understanding of three things, as blunt and unequivocal, in that instant, as the plainest of empirical facts. I understand that his power is absolute. I understand that his consciousness is distinct and individuated. Over the years, intuitively, I had grown to suspect that he or she or it was without center or form. Lastly, I understand that he explicitly decided, for reasons that are not revealed, to spare the lives of this woman and this child. I do not feel anything, associated with this presence, that might be described as boundless compassion. If he loves, I do not know. For what may well be my own limitations, I can feel nothing but his power and his will. I do not know why he spared them, but I realize that in the course of my life I have never before known the emotion of gratitude. At this moment I know nothing else. The gratitude rises and rises and rises until it is not part of me, but I of it. I have never before prayed, but I pray now. You have spared them, I say silently, and I thank you. I say it over and over again.

When I finally stand, and sag back, sitting, on the edge of the bed, the presence has departed. Only the three of us remain.

part
four

Over the course of two months, from Christmas through the middle of February, I leave no fewer than a dozen phone messages for Osman, both on his answering machine and with Nikki, and receive not a word in response. "He's never here," Nikki explains in exasperation as the weeks wear on. "I never see him." I finally decide to call twice a day, every day, morning and night, until he answers the phone. This tactic produces immediate results. As ever, he is cheerful and apologetic. We arrange that I will come up to Tahoe for a long weekend toward the end of February. In recent months he has been working as safety director on a big waterfront construction project in South Lake Tahoe. He gives me directions to the site. Friday, we confirm, about midday.

I arrive at the site as agreed, after a three-hour drive. "Embassy Vacation Resort," reads the sign. "Distinctive Vacation Ownership." Osman is nowhere to be found. "He took off around eleven," says the foreman. "I think he might have gone ice climbing." I contact Nikki at home. He left no message, and she knows nothing of his whereabouts.

Designed to resemble an old alpine hotel, the structure is

eight stories high and broad. Its steeply peaked, paneled steel roof is painted a soft grey-green to resemble weathered copper. From a distance, in comparison to the apocalyptic structures in its environs—a McDonald's directly adjacent, an International House of Pancakes across the street—the building will possess a certain grandeur. Across Route 50, groomed white ski slopes rise between the trees.

Hydraulic lifts bear workers to the building's eaves. Others, roped to safety cables on the peak above, lean back in their harnesses on the steep roof. Greg Bowler, the roofing company's project manager, observes from the ground. Bowler wears impenetrable sunglasses and a white hard hat, flanged sharply around its brim like the Allied helmets of World War I. Bowler hired Osman as safety director on the project for his knowledge of ropes and rigging. Following a system of Osman's design, the roofing company has spent more than $40,000 on safety equipment alone, including climbing rope, static line, harnesses, carabiners, and other hardware. "This is the biggest project going down in Tahoe," says Bowler. Upon completion, the resort's apartments will be marketed as time-share vacation units. Buyers may secure two weeks annually for the rest of their lives. Twenty-six owners will track through each apartment every year.

After a pass through the unfinished ground floor—teams of electricians, carpenters, and plumbers toiling in a fog of sanded plaster—I drive to Sprout's in search of Osman, or of clues to his whereabouts. A national snowboarding competition is in progress, and the café, ever a favorite of the downhill crowd, is packed to near-standing capacity. Tables spill into the adjacent gift shop. Behind the counter, four young women—including Nikki's sister Amy—prepare sandwiches, salads, and burritos with the clipped, deliberate urgency of combat medics after a shelling. When business is slow, the cooks—who all socialize outside of work—chat continuously. Now, except for the infrequent clarification of an order, they say not a word. Their expressions are flat, alternatively stern or serene. The dishes appear rhythmically on the finished pine counter, or sail out on trays through the crowd.

No one at Sprout's has seen Osman, but Amy is hosting a birthday party for a coworker late this evening—six hours hence—and Osman is expected to appear. In the meantime, Amy directs me to Maliska, working as a carpenter's apprentice in Meyers. Maliska, when I find him, suspects that Osman went ice climbing with Jason Kuchnicki. If so, he says, they commonly climb until well after dark, under headlamps, and might not return until midnight.

Continuing to Osman's house, I find it empty. I sit in my car for a time and contemplate my options. It is possible, I suppose, that Osman has consciously neglected our meeting. But I know him better than that—or think I do—and the truth, I believe, is more distressing. I believe he simply forgot.

I decide to wait him out, and motor aimlessly back into South Lake Tahoe. If I can't locate him by tomorrow morning, I'll move on.

Directly across the street from California, on either side of

Route 50, hotel casinos rise like keeps from the sidewalks. I cross the Nevada border and park in the packed lot behind Harrah's.

While not a compulsive gambler—I have never bought a lotto ticket, and have little faith that any fortune, material or otherwise, will enter my life by pure chance—I am always a sucker for a game. The attraction is largely an aesthetic one. The clacking of backgammon in cavernous Athenian cafés, and the slick marble touch of the medallions, give far more satisfaction than the simple tactics of the game itself. There is pleasure in the design and feel of playing cards, hard-edged or frayed, and the particular optimism with which a gambler fans his hand, under the clockwise pressure of his thumb, at every round of draw poker, as if granted, in those five cards, the prospect of another life.

After one, depressing look at the inside of Harrah's casino, however, I decide to forgo a few rounds of blackjack and return to Sprout's. The après-ski dinner rush is now in full swing, and the shifts have turned over. Nikki works in Amy's place. There is still no sign of Osman. Coral sits at the counter with her snowboarding instructor and a pair of friends. She stepped into a snowboard for the first time in November and was catching air on her first day. She began competing soon thereafter and has medaled in seven out of eight competitions, earning four golds, two silvers, and a bronze. This record has earned her a standing of first place in the United States of America Snowboarding Association's (USASA) Northern California/Nevada region and qualifies her to compete in the Nationals in March. She has already secured two clothing and equipment sponsors. At the end of her first season, she will go on to win the gold at the nationals for her gender and age group.

At nine-thirty I arrive at the party, already in full swing at the red A-frame shared by Amy and two roommates in South Lake Tahoe. A silver keg of ale, bathed in yellow light, stands in the subfreezing temperatures on the rear deck. A woodstove steams in the living room. Jimi Hendrix's "Red House" wails from the loft, an area partitioned by translucent, multicolored tapestries. A fifth of Jack Daniel's stands on the kitchen counter, and a pint of Jägermeister—a medicinally flavored aperitif of peppermint, licorice, and something like coal tar shampoo—reclines in the freezer. A balance of men and women, the two dozen guests are predominantly in their early to mid-twenties. With rare exception, the men are dressed in the voluminous habit favored by snowboarders. Two lean on canes, a third on a crutch—all the result of snowboarding accidents. One of them, a thirty-one-year-old carpenter, took a twenty-foot vertical drop and blew out the ligaments of one knee. The resulting surgery cost $15,000. To his relief—he and his girlfriend have an eight-month-old baby—all but $750 of this sum was paid by a state medical agency.

At ten o'clock there is still no sign of Osman. Eight or nine adolescents appear in the doorway and crowd into the main room. They claim invitations, but no one knows them, and Amy's roommate finally shepherds them out the door. Maliska appears soon after. Staggering drunk on his arrival, he is soon break dancing, after a fashion, on the wet kitchen linoleum.

At eleven o'clock Osman and Kuchnicki come through the door. Most of the guests have been drinking steadily for more than an hour—the energy in the house has mounted to a near din. In his canary-yellow down jacket, his face deeply tanned, Osman wades over to me, shakes my hand, and apologizes. He had been expecting to meet me when he left for work that morning, he claims, but forgot the appointment entirely at the suggestion of ice climbing. As a child, Osman once told me, he earned the nickname "Danny-I-forgot" from his mother and aunts. With affectionate frustration, his friends speak of the perils of operating on "Dano time," the wildly unpredictable workings of Osman's inner clock. In any case, his regret is so apparently sincere that I find myself feeling more sympathy for Osman's forgetfulness than personal offense at its effects.

Maliska's behavior continues to degenerate until he begins to playfully harass Amy's female roommates. After several warnings, at Amy's request, Osman hustles him outside and drives him home. The crowd gradually disperses, and I make my own exit shortly after two in the morning. I drive to a residential street nearby and park in the shadows. I have erected a home-made cot in the car. Composed of three lengths of particleboard bound together, the cot stretches from the dashboard to the rear platform, supported near its middle by the headrest of the reclined passenger seat. The clearance is not generous—if I lie on my side my shoulder abuts the upholstered roof—but it is comfortable enough, cushioned with an inflatable pad and blanket. In my expedition sleeping bag, suitable to twenty below, I will be amply warm. Osman, as always, has offered me his couch, but I don't want to abuse the invitation. I could always find a motel, but I have never minded sleeping in the car—to some degree, I have always enjoyed it. Every car, after a while, becomes a world unto itself, and there are few spiritual privacies like those found at the wheel of an automobile, alone, on nearly any road at four in the morning. Soon after we met, in the evenings after a date, Erin and I would usually sit for an hour or so across the street from her house, shaded by the trees from the streetlight. We talked, for the most part. For the first time, in that car, I reached out with my hand, touched her bare throat, and nearly lost consciousness. After a youth—for my part—of hit-and-run love affairs, our early courtship possessed an extraordinary innocence.

In South Lake Tahoe I crack the windows, cram myself into my bookshelf of a bed, and fidget, finally, into a comfortable position. This is the first night, I realize suddenly, that I have spent apart from my family since Julia's birth.

Last Thanksgiving weekend, while visiting Julia's aunt and uncle in suburban Reno, Nevada, Julia smiled for the first time. There is much talk, in pediatric literature, of gastrointestinal "smiles" versus real smiles and the difficulty of distinguishing one from the other. In Julia's case, her occasional, indigestive grimace in no way resembled an emotive grin. And although we had agreed not to speak of it—not to pressure her with requests—it was becoming increasingly difficult, on some level, not to know if our daughter was happy. She seemed perfectly content, in the sense that she rarely cried, and never inconsolably. But she had never shown what could clearly be interpreted as amusement or pleasure. She merely gazed at us with what appeared to be mild, noncommittal curiosity. Some objects, like the white Christmas lights strung in arcs along the eaves of our bedroom, gripped her within days of her birth. She stared at the lights with her dark newborn eyes with a fascination—touched with horror—so profound that we in turn gazed at her dumbstruck. Hers was the expression that one might expect to have seen on Saul's face as he lay in the sand outside Damascus, unhorsed. I do not know if she became aware, as she stared at these lights for the first time, that she could see. Or if she herself became, in those moments, "pointed brightness in a field of grey," in the way, when we are deep in grief, that we become that grief. In any case, something in her had changed. From a behavioral standpoint it would doubtless be considered "development," but whether it was something made or broken I cannot say. Part of me suspected that in apprehending the world, as in being named, she had been driven further aground on mortal shoals. Don't come in, a voice within me tried to warn her, and too late, in her first, ephemeral days. You are perfect now. Do not trade perfection for the narrow, treacherous confines of a human life.

The fall after Erin and I graduated from college we moved to the woods in upstate New York and lived through the winter in near seclusion. The phone would go days without ringing. We snuck into town like spies once every week or ten days for groceries. We took long walks, returning with the dusk, and read late into the night in the warm kitchen, side by side in front of the woodstove. It was so flawless a time that even as I observed it, unfolding, spending itself, day upon day, I was aware of its perfection. This, I told myself, is a perfect life. I tried, but could find no argument. One night, as we lay in the darkness—we were not even engaged, and our wedding was three years hence—I had an unbidden, catastrophic understanding that even in the best of circumstances we would have only one life together. In the temporal foreshortening of that late hour, deep in the woods of midwinter, it was like learning that one of us—it hardly mattered who—was jammed to the marrow with cancer. I lost all perspective; it felt as if Erin would be taken from me at daybreak, and I wasn't ready to surrender her.

The next day I woke in better spirits, and our life, returning to its ordinary proportions, was just as before. But the understanding left an enduring mark, a chill that has never quite lifted. Now there is the vaguest sense that Erin and I, in giving form to Julia, have betrayed her. At five months her perfection still gleams on her like scales. But we have locked her with ourselves into our time, and there is no reversal.

In her aunt's house outside Reno, Julia—then seven weeks old—had slept beside our bed in the bottom drawer of a mahogany dresser, set on the floor like a cradle and padded with towels, blankets, and pillowcases. When she woke we took her into bed and laid her between us. Eventually, Erin left the room to take a shower. The water drummed across the hallway. The rest of the house was asleep. The blind beside the bed was drawn, but the light came around the edges of the shade and illuminated the white trim. Thus reflected, it cast a diffused glow about the room. Julia lay on her back, bundled in her blanket, in a knit cap. I lay beside her, my head up on an elbow, talking to her quietly, and she smiled, casually, broadly, with her entire face. I stared, afraid to speak or move. She smiled again. I wanted to shout for Erin but was afraid to break the spell. I held my breath. She smiled a third time, a slow, beautifully toothless smile.

I have wondered what it would be like to be present when a loved one wakes from a coma after many months or years. It was as if, after an interminable silence, Julia was answering the question: Will you accept this life? Will you accept us, who know we are inadequate? Will you know joy? These are all questions, bound of a piece, that hang unanswered in those early weeks. Yes, she answered, finally, with her smile. Yes. And the covenant—between us and her, between her and her own life, much of which she will live beyond our longest reach—was sealed. It was Thanksgiving Day.

.   .   .

I wake in the car suddenly, to daylight and hushed voices. I open my eyes and meet the gaze of a small boy, peering through the car's rear window from the seat of his bicycle. He jumps. Behind him is another boy, looking over his shoulder. They lunge away from the car, giggling, and pedal down the street as if pursued. Soon after, Osman and I convene at Maliska's. Osman wants to go ice climbing, but Maliska, his face ashen, declines. "I'm not feeling too chippewah," he says. Kuchnicki, too, is unavailable.

After a late lunch at Sprout's, Osman and I drive out to Emerald Bay. The parking lot is snowed in, and Osman parks along the side of the two-lane highway, within sight of the marbled Mayhem wall. We gear up and hike south in our packs, along the road, its shoulders walled with four-foot drifts of snow. Two hundred yards south of the truck, Osman glances in both directions—it is illegal to climb at the site because of avalanche danger—and turns off the road uphill. He follows a trail of steps in the snow up the steep hillside into the pines.

Five minutes from the highway, through the trees, a wall of quartz-monzonite, or granite, rises from the snow. The salt-and-pepper coloring of granite comes from these two minerals; the white is quartz, the black monzonite. A soaring seventy-foot column of vertical blue ice clings to the wall. The column, known as the Inertia Tube, is the closest decent ice climbing to South Lake Tahoe. To the left of the column, the rock slightly overhangs. To the right, the wall is coated with a crystal veneer of ice, little more than an inch thick, the texture of the stone visible beneath it. The Inertia Tube is born and nourished every year by a trickling stream of snowmelt from the peaks far above. Two days ago, ten feet from the edge of the cliff, Osman built a stone dam in the stream. Lining the dam with plastic bags to form a pool, he diverted a portion of the flow into a ³/₈-inch-diameter rubber hose, positioning its mouth atop the bare, vertical rock to the right of the Tube. The resulting icefall is sixty feet high and some fifteen feet wide. Osman inspects the growing ice—still too fine to climb—with parental satisfaction. Near its base, the ice clings to the stone like a lattice of clear, interlocking glass marbles. He taps the ice lightly with the pick of his tool. "Tomorrow," he says.

We lay out our gear in an existing camp, a broad, flat bench of snow stomped into the slope beneath the lower branches of a pine. Cigarette butts lie scattered in the camp's environs. Beyond the bench, at the base of a tree, the snow has recently been punctured with urine. Soon, in his bright red and yellow and black regalia, with ice screws dangling from the loops of his harness, rigid crampons strapped to his purple plastic boots, a headlamp on his red helmet, and his ice tools—objects of sinister, efficient beauty—in his gloved hands, he is ready to climb. The manufacturers' bellicose names for Osman's crampons and tools—Switchblades and Predators, respectively—are representative of the field.

Positioned in crampons and helmet, comfortably entombed in Osman's expedition-weight down jacket, I will belay from behind the relative shelter of a low rock wall to the left of the Inertia Tube. Should a large shard of ice cut loose overhead, freed from the column by Osman's tools or front-points, I may duck left, behind the wall and out of the missile's path. The down jacket—known affectionately by Osman and his associates as the Sleeping Bag—has arms the diameter of volleyballs and is worn gratefully by whoever is belaying. While ice climbing well into the evening, as is Osman's wont, the temperatures drop at an alarming pace, and the belayer, standing more or less motionless for periods of half an hour or more, needs all the insulation technology can afford.

Through the trees to the east I discern the island, crowned by its ruined castle, in the middle of Emerald Bay. At this desolate hour, under a windless winter sky, the bay is abandoned, unruffled, the color of slate. In the world in this guise, in these expectant, trembling tones of grey, I feel most at ease. Seasonally, I am happiest in late October. Not so in spring; I am sickened, inexplicably, by the sight of new green thrusting from the mud between patches of exhausted snow.

I do not know to what degree Osman shares this sentiment, but I am intensely uncomfortable in crowds. The most pleasing sound to my ear—with the exception, now, of the baby's long, kettling sigh, produced intermittently while she sleeps—is the percussion of rain falling like gunshots, hammering, battering like a vengeful god, upon a flat, uninsulated roof in an all-but-empty house on an island—a true island, mind, unconnected by bridges—in the off-season.

During my first year in France, now nearly a decade past, I often found my way to the cemeteries of Montmartre and Père Lachaise. In the autumn months, especially, the golden chestnut leaves gathering on the headstones and upon the bricks, I walked through these graveyards, reading the stones, and my spirit gradually filled with a clear, exuberant joy. I was sometimes accompanied on these walks by a female companion, and in these majestically still environments one kiss could scorch the senses like a pillar of fire. With the myopic shamelessness of youth, we would soon move to the modest shelter afforded between a pair of mausoleums, or a stone-walled corner, shielded by trees. Thus concealed, her embraces told me that I would never lie amongst those others, there, beneath the stones.

· · ·

I t is five-thirty before Osman places his first tool with a consid-

ered swing following three gentle, preparatory pecks. With the
rope secured to his harness, he solos a rounded, ten-foot bulge at
the base of the column. At the sloping top of the bulge he pauses
to stretch his back and legs. Extending one leg and then the
other, he touches the brim of his helmet to each knee. When he
finally starts up the vertical column, his pace is markedly more
reflective than it was at Kirkwood nearly two years before. At
Kirkwood, free-soloing shorter icefalls, Osman moved with an
easy flamboyance. Here, he is leading a longer, more difficult
route, under inferior light, and must spend his energy with care.
He is older, more skilled, his style now closer to Jay Smith's.

Tick, tick, tick, tick—he pecks patiently at a depression in
the ice with the sharp pick of his right-hand tool. Swinging
from the wrist, he allows the weight of the tool's head to do
much of the work. With each swing the pick drives deeper into
the slot, forming a sheath in the ice. As he works, almost all of
his weight rests on the front-points of his crampons, level beneath him. He stands easily, knees straight but not locked, as if
on a stone ledge. His hands are secured to his tools with wrist
straps, so designed that he may hang from them, while weighting the tools, without tightly gripping their shafts. Novices commonly fail by overgripping their tools, swiftly exhausting the
muscles of their forearms. While he swings with his right, Osman's left hand rests in its wrist strap, unweighted, barely grip-

ping the shaft of his tool. If, by chance, his front-points were to shear out, Osman's weight would be supported by the left-hand tool. In the meantime, it serves only to help keep him upright.

Having prepared the slot, Osman sets the right-hand tool in place with a sharp swing, powered by the wrist and elbow. The bottom edge of the tool's pick is serrated with teeth that grip the ice and prevent slippage. In places, where the ice allows, picks may be rested in large, natural slots without swinging. Used correctly, such placements save both energy and time. Osman places his left tool, then moves up with his feet. He jerks his right crampon loose, inspects the ice a foot above his last placement, and throws a series of firm kicks at his target. Not intended to adhere, these blows prepare the surface, chipping off layers of brittle, wind-chilled surface ice to reveal the dense, plastic ice that lies centimeters beneath. This ice, as much as several degrees warmer than the surface layer, is much less likely to shatter under Osman's kicks or shear beneath his weight. Satisfied, Osman plants the crampon with a last, concentrated kick; he will not shift it again, even slightly, until ready to remove it. Now eight feet above the base of the column, he stems wide with his left foot, bracing straight-legged against the overhanging stone. So secured, he loosens one tool, letting it dangle from its wrist strap, and places his first piece of protection—a six-inch ice screw—with his freed hand. He clips a carabiner to the hanger on the screw's head and clips his rope into the carabiner. He retracts his left leg from the wall, places the crampon beside its mate, and looks overhead for his next placements. He does not look far—overextension, in ice as in rock climbing, disrupts the climber's balance; the time it promises to save is illusory.

Beginning rock climbers almost invariably reach far over their heads for distant holds, rising on their toes and laying their bodies flat upon the rock. As they gain experience, they learn to keep their weight upright, over their feet, and to keep their hands on holds, for the most part, within a comfortable reach. Indeed, the best climbers often ascend entire routes with their hands rarely rising far above the level of their shoulders. They will look for handholds anywhere within the circular area of terrain, some six feet in diameter, accessible at any point in time by their two hands, and not simply along that circle's northern rim.

When Osman sees a potential placement, he extracts the right-hand tool, pulling up and down on the base of the shaft until the slot widens enough to release the pick. Tool, tool—foot, foot, Osman methodically scales the column. He pauses infrequently to place protection—a total of three screws on the seventy-foot climb—each time stemming to the rock with his left foot. As he climbs, chunks of ice rain down sporadically. Most of it deflects harmlessly away, down the slope, but now and then a shard will angle off in my direction. I lean left toward the wall and lower my helmeted head as the chip whirs past. Thanks to my defensive placement, I am struck only once in the course of Osman's climb. A piece of ice the size of a golf ball raps the crown of my plastic helmet and ricochets off into the trees.

At six-fifteen, forty-five minutes after leaving the ground, Osman is three-quarters of the way through the climb. So little natural light remains that all the color has drained from his clothing—the brilliant reds and yellows are now greys. At the moment I observe this, Osman turns on his headlamp. A yellow cone of light sweeps across the ice over his head, and then, as he looks down, between his boots, spills to the base of the column and sets alight the droplets of moisture that cling to the count less knobs and promontories of ice. The sudden appearance of the artificial light, while fantastic in its effects, deepens and finalizes the moonless darkness. Outside the lamp's narrow range, the ice, the rock, the trees, are now featureless fields, wedges, and slashes of charcoal and pitch against the pale plane—the nonspace, unfathomable to the eyes in such a light—that I know to be snow.

The air is getting colder. While the atmosphere within the parka is comfortably temperate, my toes are losing circulation fast. I burrow them futilely into twin layers of Capilene and wool. My old, beloved leather boots, well suited to a sunlit ascent of Shasta, are inadequate to the present task.

Osman tops out at six-thirty, and the cone of light vanishes with him. As my vision adjusts I make out stars, dimly, in an overcast sky. "Off belay," Osman hollers finally. "Thank you," I call, and untie from the rope. Minutes later, having set a top-rope anchor for my ascent, Osman and his lamp reappear over the edge and he begins his rappel, pausing to clean his protection from the ice as he descends. Having crossed to the other side of the column to be clear of ice fall, I cannot see Osman as he tinkers with a screw, but his small, dying lamp penetrates the ice—hollow where the water runs at its core—defracts against the countless crystal faces locked within, and illuminates the seventy-foot column like a pillar of blue flame, a marbled aquamarine that shifts and ripples with the faintest movements of the climber's chin.

Safe on the ground, unclipping from his rappel, Osman rates his freshly completed route up the pillar's left side as a 5+ or 6, roughly equivalent to 5.10 or .11 in rock climbing. Although the Inertia Tube is a short piece for such a high rating—many of the most challenging icefalls are hundreds of feet in height—Osman awards the rating for technical difficulty. In places, clinging to the angled rock behind it, the ice slightly overhangs.

Osman offers me his tools and crampons in exchange for the Sleeping Bag. He dons the jacket quickly, before the heat entrapped within is lost. While climbing, my pile sweater and wind shell will be more than adequate. On top rope, I will attempt the standard route up the Tube's right flank. The route, says Osman, is a low 4+, the approximate equivalent of a rock climbing 5.8 or .9. I am short on sleep, my feet are cold, and I am lethargic from the long belay. The last time I climbed vertical ice was over a year ago, with Greenwell in upstate New York, and as I step into Osman's crampons I feel decidedly uninspired. Ice tools in hand, standing at the pillar's base, I lean back and sweep my headlamp up the column's length. In an unambitious frame of mind, at night, seventy feet of vertical ice looks like a long way.

Following Osman's example, I do not hurry. I conserve arm strength by hooking, where possible, instead of swinging the tools. The Predators are better balanced, and grip the ice with greater tenacity, than models I have used on prior climbs. When I do swing, the picks seat firmly with little effort. As I ascend, I take particular care to avoid slashing the blue-checked rope in my path. An 8.5-millimeter "dry" rope, it has been chemically treated to retard water. A standard, untreated rope exposed to snow and ice will quickly become waterlogged, gaining pounds in weight and, as temperatures drop, freezing into the consistency of steel cable. For a party of exhausted climbers descending a peak in rapidly degenerating weather, a rime-encrusted rope that cannot be managed can spell a grim conclusion to the climb.

Thinner than a standard rope, the 8.5-millimeter cord on the Inertia Tube is called a half-rope or double rope, as it is often used, when belaying a leader on technical sections of ice or rock, in conjunction with a second rope of the same diameter. For roping together on glaciers and light belaying, many alpine climbers favor half-ropes for their inferior weight. Averaging six and a half pounds, a sixty-meter half-rope weighs on average two pounds less than a 10.5-millimeter rope of the same length. Two pounds may seem negligible at sea level, but it is revealing to note that some mountaineers, while paring down equipment for an expedition, snap their toothbrushes in half and hollow out the bristled end with a drill bit to reduce weight. This may appear compulsive, even superstitious, but when applied to a climber's entire load, fractions of ounces rapidly accumulate to pounds. Over the course of a major climb, ounces are minutes, minutes are hours, and hours, in the end, may be life to a climber at high altitude. To ascend from base camp to the summit of Everest, the average, superbly conditioned climber will burn between 5,000 and 6,000 calories per day, the average expenditure of a Maine lumberman in midwinter.

For my top rope on the Inertia Tube, the single 8.5 is more than adequate to sustain a fall. A more conservative climber, however, might feel uncomfortable *leading* the column, as Osman did earlier, on the same rope.

Enamored with the tools, concentrating on their application, I soon discover that I am neglecting my feet, as I did at Kirkwood with Osman two years before. I catch myself, in places, scratching with the crampons for purchase, overweighting my wrist straps, and high-stepping onto skull-sized bulges rather than consistently placing my front-points. Osman encourages me to concentrate on my feet, and I do so, improving apace. I make surprisingly steady progress and am soon invigorated, determined to top out. At fifty feet I swing left with a thoughtless, investigative peck into a large bulge of ice on the column's prow. This was a mistake; convex surfaces will usually "dinnerplate," or shear away in flattish shards, when struck by the pick. Sure enough, a fissure shoots vertically from the pick in both directions, and an irregular block of ice the size of a twenty-one-inch television cuts loose from the column and sails to earth. "Ice," I call redundantly. Osman, well to the right of the column, bows his head to shelter his face. The berg slams into the bulge at the column's base and explodes with a flat boom. There is a pause as the debris skitters down the slope of crusted snow. "Waaaah," I call down apologetically. Osman is unscathed. "You probably want to avoid those bulges," he says.

Three times during the ascent I pause to rest. I do not weight the rope but stand on my front-points, gently grasping the tools. I remind myself to loosen my grip, to trust the tools, to concentrate on my feet, and most of all to take my time. Ten feet from the top, I come upon a window in the ice, eighteen inches across, through which I can inspect the Tube's interior. I cast my light within. Water courses down the inside walls.

Half an hour after starting the climb, I hook the exposed root of a shrub emerging from the snow near the cliff's edge and move over the lip onto flat ground. I rise to my feet, still belayed, with a great surge of satisfaction. Unmotivated at the column's base, I hadn't expected to finish the climb. Now—energized, relaxed, the chill lifted from my toes—I could happily climb well into the night. I move clear of the edge, untie from the rope, and call to Osman, "Off belay."

Fifteen feet from the lip, to my surprise, the rope is anchored to a tree trunk, some six inches in diameter, with a single, wire-gated carabiner on a sling. The anchor is an exercise in minimalism, and my enthusiasm is cut by a retroactive bleed of unease. If I had seen the anchor Osman placed, I would not have attempted the route.

Given his proclivity toward falling, Osman knows the actual capacities of climbing ropes and hardware as well as or better, I imagine, than any other climber alive. He is clearly confident in the accuracy of this knowledge, for he repeatedly wagers his life and the lives of others on its basis. As an intermediate climber with a general mistrust of things man-made, I am in no position to question Osman's understanding of climbing gear, of its strengths and limitations. But I have been taught differently, over the years, by climbers—less skilled than Osman, certainly, but in many cases older—who while setting anchors insisted on as many redundancies as time and circumstance could reasonably afford. In setting a top rope, for example—although one carabiner, one sling, and one cam in a sound crack could theoretically hold most conceivable falls—most climbers commonly demand a minimum of three or four equalized pieces for the anchor to be considered absolutely reliable, or bomb-proof.

For Osman, it appears, an anchor is either adequate or inadequate. This seems to be an issue of aesthetics rather than bravado, reminiscent of his response to my suggestion of a backup for my jump at Cave Rock. If Osman knows, through extensive experience, that X alone is more than enough to safely protect a given route, it would be gratuitous, and thus wasteful, to protect the route with $X + X + X$. In pursuit of mastery in any enterprise, one strives to attain or express a condition *just so,* and chasms of mediocrity—too much and not enough—yawn on either side. By this reasoning, one might argue, superfluous gear on a top-rope anchor is not a harmless, sensible backup, but as regrettable—to borrow from another trade—as an overwritten phrase.

Some of this, to be sure, may derive from the varying degree of ethical and legal responsibility dictated by the relationship of the climbers in question. Some—but not all—of the climbers who emphasized, in my presence, the necessity of three- and four-piece top-rope anchors were instructors, officially responsible for their clients' welfare. This evening, on the other hand, I am climbing as Osman's peer, despite the gross inequity of skill. This is neither a class nor a guided climb; we are climbing, in effect, in the real world.

I worked for a time as an assistant scuba instructor, and we impressed upon our students the absolute inflexibility of these and other dictums: always ascend at a tank pressure greater than or equal to five hundred pounds; never descend, as a recreational diver on compressed air, below a depth of 130 feet (this limit was proscribed for advanced divers; novices were cautioned to remain above a depth of 60 feet); and most important: never, ever dive alone. As a beginning diver—while a freshman in college—I had scrupulously observed these laws. I was led to believe that all divers, my instructors included, observed them, and that any who did not were dangerous incompetents. On my first dive from the deck of an overnight charter boat, however (my first foray beyond the company of other, identically earnest beginners), every diver aboard—including my ostensible partner and erstwhile assistant instructor—sank into the water alone. Out of some fifteen veteran divers—I was the sole novice aboard—I don't believe a single "buddy team" left the boat. I glanced at the impassive divemaster, appalled, before I understood. And off I went, alone, into the depths. In the aquatic California wilderness afforded by the boat's great range, the diving was spectacular. That night, around the galley tables, I heard tell of Japanese warplanes on the floors of lagoons in Micronesia, of tiger shark attacks repelled with bang sticks, of dives, on compressed air, to depths approaching three hundred feet. These divers, I believed, were the sport's hard core. Later, when it came my turn to teach, I held up the side. Never, ever dive alone, I echoed. It was a sham of sorts, a double standard. But it was better, we believed, than the alternative.

After cleaning Osman's anchor and inspecting his diversion dam, I follow the trail through the snow, circling back and around to the base of the wall. Osman shakes my hand, offering praise for my performance. As we break down our gear and pack up, I inquire about the reliability of the anchor. Osman answers that a veteran ice climber had previously challenged the same anchor, on the same climb, and that his answer to him was the same: given the extreme friction generated by the rounded slope of snow and ice, and the distance from the tree to the edge, a belayer standing beside the tree could hold a top-rope fall from the column with one hand. A single carabiner and sling, therefore, was more than adequate to hold a similar fall. Perhaps, I conceded, but what about the possibility of the rope looping back over the carabiner's gate and unclipping itself, a common danger normally safeguarded through the use of two carabiners, placed side by side with opposing gates? (Alternatively, a locking carabiner may be used, its gate secured with a manually operated retractable cuff.) Osman admits that a locker would be easy enough to substitute but that the distance from the edge to the anchor prevents the rope from looping over the gate. If the anchor had been closer to the lip, he says, where the movements of the rope were less predictable, he would certainly have used a locker. In any case, Osman agrees to place an extra carabiner for me on future climbs.

For my part, I feel somewhat ungrateful for raising the issue. Nevertheless, we hike through the trees in good spirits and turn down the road into a rising wind. Dense spindrifts of snow whirl and dance in the light of our headlamps. When we turn off the lamps, the broad-peaked ridge above the Mayhem wall dominates the sky, a black curtain streaked with snowbound gullies of grey. Far across the lake, to the east, the lights of human settlements gleam dully. We hike into the facing wind. For the moment, I have forgotten the anchor. There is only the wind, the deep cold, and the climbing—the memory of its rhythm lingering in my limbs—and at the moment I feel nothing but the profound contentment of the living.

After a late dinner at Sprout's, Osman and I part ways at eleven o'clock. I retire to a ramshackle motel in Meyers. It is a gloomy, inhospitable cell, with no phone, a broken gas heater, and a splintered door that does not lock from within. In the wailing wind, forty-eight hours since my last shower, I thought better of the cot in the car. After wedging a chair under the doorknob to keep the wind from battering the door ajar, I spend half an hour in the nearly unbearable heat of the shower, dozing upright with my head against the tiles.

By seven o'clock the following morning, the snow is falling fine and hard. An inch of powder, dry as volcanic ash, covers the ground. I soon make my way to Osman's, as agreed.

Late in the morning, hurrying to pay rent, Nikki loses

control of her car on Route 50—at the Sawmill turnoff for the Pie Shop—spins down the road, and hurtles sideways into a six-foot ditch. The vehicle misses a telephone pole by an armspan and slams into an inflexible steel fence. Instants after coming to rest, nearly incoherent with fear, she calls Osman at home by cell phone. "Accident . . . Nikki," he mumbles frantically, and sprints for his truck. I follow in my car and soon come upon the scene. Nikki is terrified but unhurt. The car is totaled. Given the conditions, heavy traffic, fixed obstacles, and the state of her car after the accident, her escape from injury is nearly miraculous. Just moments before losing control, she had remembered to buckle her seat belt.

After helping make arrangements for the car, a slow day follows for Osman, much of it spent on the couch at Maliska's. The sun reappears; the snow melts from the roads. At six o'clock in the evening, Osman, Maliska, and I join a gathering of some eighteen Tahoe-area climbers on the floor of a local gymnastic and climbing gym to discuss the recent closing of Cave Rock. Despite opposition from local climbers and the Access Fund, a national nonprofit organization dedicated to preserving climbers' access to established climbing areas, the U.S. Forest Service has temporarily closed the cave at the request of the local Washo Indian tribe. Religious figures in the tribe still consider the cave sacred and have decided—after decades of neglect—to reclaim it as their own. The presence of the climbers and their hardware, they argue, is blasphemous. There is rumor of a land deal: in exchange for the cave, the Forest Service may receive an appetizing parcel of Washo land elsewhere in the region.

The climbers, naturally enough, are incensed. Osman alone has put years of work into the cave; it represents a gallery of his finest work. The cave is also the only year-round extreme sport climbing area in the Tahoe region. Largely for the quality of Osman's lines, the cave is a world climbing destination. As it stands, however, the cave is closed to climbers until further review, at the least until the end of the year. In the meantime—a period of nine months—any climber apprehended on the walls of the cave will suffer a $5,000 fine. In the worst-case scenario, every bolt on every route will eventually be chopped by the Forest Service, climbing at the cave forever banned.

With the help of the Access Fund, the climbers agree to sustain pressure on the Forest Service. Emotion in the meeting runs high. Some of the climbers question the Washos' motives and accuse the Forest Service of corruption. Osman, who of all the company stands most to lose from the closure, remains composed. "The Washo had their time in the cave," he says. "This is our time. When we started climbing there, the cave was a mess—full of beer bottles and diapers and garbage. Where were the Washo then? We cleaned it up, and we treat it with respect. The Washo say it's a spiritual place for them. But it's a spiritual place for us, too. Anyone who climbs can understand that." He declares his intention to meet with the Washo themselves. "I have a good feeling," he says. "Once they understand how we feel about the cave, I think we can work something out."

After the meeting we are joined at Maliska's by Frank Gambalie, a mutual acquaintance and prominent Bay Area BASE jumper. BASE (building, antenna, span, and earth) jumpers leap—often clandestinely, facing arrest and fines—from terrestrially fixed structures or natural formations with a specialized parachute. The sport kills a proportionately higher number of participants than skydiving because the reduced heights are much less forgiving of equipment failures, or split-second errors in judgment. In the shortest BASE jumps, there is no time to throw a backup chute should the primary fail. Stylistically, the ideal BASE jump is executed in broad daylight from a prominent, dramatic location—the Golden Gate Bridge, for example, or the Eiffel Tower—perforce illegally. In some cases, the jumper slips literally through the lunging hands of authorities and taunts them with a gesture as he falls. He throws his chute at the last possible moment before landing and effecting his escape.

Gambalie, twenty-six at the time of our meeting, has made nearly five hundred jumps in six countries, including a 6,700-foot, twenty-six-second plunge from the Trollveggen cliff in Norway, the world record. Osman has many of Gambalie's greatest coups on videotape, including his record leap and a comic urban sequence in which the jumper vaults 600 feet from a skyscraper in Frankfurt, Germany. With accomplices waiting on the ground, Gambalie lands in a small grassy lot and jumps into the backseat of a waiting car without shedding his chute. As the car speeds off, he gathers the billowing white folds of his nylon chute into the car after him like the train of a bridal gown. Gambalie's reputation for fearlessness rivals or exceeds Osman's own, in their overlapping circles, and Osman's admiration for the BASE jumper is pronounced.

Gambalie later tells me that Osman is a born BASE jumper. "I haven't met anyone with Dano's talent and drive," he says. "He's a BASE jumper and he doesn't even know it." Osman plans to learn the sport from Gambalie and has already treated the BASE jumper to a roped bridge fall. The sensation of "ground rush"—the spectacle of the earth at close range, hurtling skyward to meet you—sought by BASE jumpers is even greater using Osman's system, Gambalie claims. On rope, a jumper can come far closer to the ground before deceleration than one dependent on a chute, or on bungee cord, which slows the faller dramatically before nearing the earth.

Gambalie got his start in the aerial arts as a bungee jumper. "With extra cord out," he recounts, "we used to jump into shallow pools between boulders in a riverbed. The pools weren't directly below the launch, so we had to aim for them— we had to glide as we fell. The pools weren't very big, and if we missed, that would have been it. 'Float or die,' we used to say. 'Float or die.'" Gambalie snickers. The audience is rapt; even Osman regards the speaker with awe. Gambalie goes on to describe a bungee-jumping variation called sandbagging—one jumper on bungee cord leaps with another clinging to him. The "sandbag" is in no way affixed to the cord, and must let go—over a deep, watery landing to prevent injury—at the lowest point of the jump. This increased weighting slingshots the secured jumper to heights exceeding the launching point. Unsurprisingly, more than one person has been killed through this practice. Bungee jumping, however, is tame fare in comparison to BASE jumping. Among Gambalie's circle of BASE-jumping acquaintances alone there have been four fatal accidents. In each case, says Gambalie, "they were absolutely competent. We all have the understanding: don't be sorry for me if I die doing what I love. It's always a huge loss, but I try to let their deaths be inspiring." Despite low participation in BASE jumping—an estimated 200 seriously pursue it worldwide—some 40 have been killed since the advent of the sport in 1970. "If you don't like funerals," Gambalie concludes, echoing the phrase often applied—and with the same dry irony—to police work, fire fighting, and other life-threatening trades, "you're in the wrong industry."

I meet Osman the following morning at the construction site. It is clear and cold—twenty-six degrees in the sun—and a stiff wind beats the surface of the lake. Osman and I don helmets and orange rescue harnesses—their hoisting D-rings, positioned at the sternum, are rated to four tons—and ride the elevator to the roof, eighty-six feet above the frozen ground. While the wind on the heights does not suit the taste of most roofers, the majority of whom have taken the day off, we find Kuchnicki and Paul Crawford—one of the region's finest ice climbers— working at the building's western prow. With many first ascents on vertical ice in the United States and Canada, Crawford recently retired from the sport at the age of thirty-eight.

While Crawford supplies roofing panels from the basket of a hydraulic lift, Kuchnicki leans back in his harness and drills the interlocking panels into position. Pulling a length of orange rope from a gang box on the roof's flattened peak, Osman clips into a safety system of static lines secured to steel struts. The fifteen-millimeter lines have a working load of nine thousand pounds and will sustain twice that—nine tons—before breaking. With an ascender and belaying device, Osman rappels down the roof to check a bolt in the system. On his return, he pats a knot securing the static line to a steel upright. "On this job, if you ever untie one of these knots, you get sent home for the day without pay. If you do it again, you're fired." The lines are placed in such a way—a central line with tributaries extending out along the spine of every eave—that a worker, anchored correctly to the system, can reach any part of the roof safely. I take a rope, clip a locking carabiner into the primary anchor line, and rappel down the roof. Nearing the edge, I begin to move laterally, letting out rope, and Osman stops me. "Stay under your anchor," he cautions. Instead of letting out line and moving diagonally away from the central line, I must climb up and transfer the carabiner to a tributary, allowing the carabiner to move with me as I sidestep along the roof.

Weeks ago, a roofer was nearly killed for this oversight. Working near the roof's edge, his rope was taut but running at an angle to the nearest union. When the roofer slipped, and pendulumed to a point beneath his carabiner, the radius of his line extended over the roof's sharp edge. The friction of his weight in the fall sawed the line nearly through against the steel panels, severing the sheath and leaving only strands of nylon core intact. He dangled, unhurt, until other workers lowered him another line.

On the roof, Osman observes that Kuchnicki's carabiner is clipped to a steel cable running parallel to the static line, and asks him to clip into the safety rope.

"It works fine," Kuchnicki protests. "I used it all day yesterday."

"The steel cable works like a cheese grater on the aluminum biner," Osman says, sawing a forefinger in the notch of his opposing hand. "If you want to use the cable, switch to a steel biner." Kuchnicki considers this for a moment and complies.

The roofers are split into five crews; the most productive of these—they log more hours and lay more steel per capita per hour—is strictly composed of South Tahoe climbers, all acquaintances of Osman's, including Kuchnicki and Crawford. The climbers are more comfortable working at these heights and with the use of Osman's safety system—derived directly as it is from climbing applications—than the other crews. Statistically, the climbers' work on-site is more dangerous than most anything they do on rock or ice.

After high school—determined, at the time, to avoid college—I worked construction off and on for a couple of years. In the sodden, hundred-degree heat of a summer outside Washington, D.C., I worked on a fencing crew for five bucks an hour, erecting chain link, among other projects, around the perimeter of a professional football stadium. Thanks to a poor bid, we worked twelve-hour days without breaking for lunch. There was not a scrap of shade within fifty yards of the fence line, and we would surreptitiously wolf down sandwiches over two or three trips to the truck for supplies. The first winter, for the same wage, I worked for a stonemason on a big waterfront project in Georgetown. We built arches from scaffolds, and one morning I made a foolish mistake. I was securing a tarp to the exterior frame of the scaffold, to protect us from the freezing rain, and a huge belly of wind rolled through the unwalled structure behind me. It filled the tarp like a spinnaker, and in an instant I was out in space, sixty feet above an unforgiving landing. I floated there, clutching the slick plastic, long enough to think about it. Will I catch the edge of the steel wheelbarrow, weighted with sand, or plow straight into the pile of stone slabs? The tarp held, fixed securely to the roof above. When the gust subsided, I swung back with a crash into the scaffold's frame and caught hold. I was terrified, but the event barely raised an eyebrow from my partners. "Watch yourself," one of them said mildly. They were all construction lifers and a good deal older than I. In construction—on big jobs in particular—any day with nothing but close calls is a good day. Over the course of his career, the mason had seen more than a score of men killed in various ways on building sites; eleven of them died in falls.

In Tahoe I drop down to a position between Crawford and Kuchnicki to observe how the roofing is installed. I pass materials between them. Above, on the roof's exposed, windswept peak, it is brutally cold. Down here, in the lee of the roof, in the sun, it is almost mild.

"It's warmer down here, out of the wind," I offer. Crawford ignores the remark. A wad of dipping tobacco rides in his cheek; he averts his chin and spits a ropy wad of coffee-colored juice into the air. Beneath a cap his hair is closely cropped. He is well over six feet tall and spare, and you could not drive a nail through the granite wall of his expression with a framing hammer. Crawford's manner has earned him the nickname "Dirty Harry" among locals. As I later learn from Kuchnicki—whom Crawford addresses as "Skippy"—Crawford considers Osman a showman. Nevertheless, gathered on the rooftop minutes later, Osman and Crawford chat amicably about the condition of local ice climbs.

Osman plans an afternoon trip to the Inertia Tube and invites Kuchnicki to join us after completing a half-day on the roof. Kuchnicki first demurs, then agrees to join us at noon.

Osman has checked the safety system and is free to go. As we emerge from the elevator on the ground floor, a worker passing in the corridor shouts, "Hey, Dano, I saw you on TV." Osman waves bashfully. No fewer than four clips of Osman climbing or jumping are now running on different cable programs. To his frustration, he is rarely notified of these appearances by the producers responsible. Instead he commonly learns of airings after the fact, from friends and even strangers. "Not once has anyone called me and said, 'Hey, Dano, I sold a piece and it's going to air on such and such a date, and here's your cut,'" he recounts. "I always have to track them down."

We inspect a time-share unit, nearing completion, on the ground floor. The paint and carpeting are finished, the bathroom attractively tiled. A wheeled combination safe stands ajar in the closet. The split-level ceiling is decorated with mock beams. Above the beams, in an attempt at Santa Fe, rounds of pine emerge from the wall. The structural depth they suggest is illusory; the rounds are glued like soup cans to the finished wall.

While we wait for Kuchnicki to finish his shift, Osman and I cross Route 50 to the pancake house.

"Jason is really my next hopeful," says Osman over a late breakfast. "He's the fastest-improving ice climber I've ever seen. Within one month of taking it up, he's following a five." Osman praises Kuchnicki's humility and his eagerness to learn.

A woman in early middle age tentatively approaches our table. "Excuse me," she says, "did I see you on television?" Osman smiles, shrugs. "It's possible," he answers. "Yeah, it's definitely you," she says. "I told my husband it was you." She gestures to a man in a distant booth, who waves. Hailing from Suisun City, fifty miles west of Sacramento, the couple are in town to ski, and to attend their daughter's wedding, at the same chapel in which they themselves were married. Last night in their hotel room, the woman explains, they stumbled across a program of Osman jumping and free-soloing. "We were so impressed," she says. "I could never imagine doing that."

"It's just what I do," says Osman. "If you put me in your job, I'm sure I'd feel exactly the same way."

"Do you get scared, doing those things?" she asks him.

"Yeah," he says. "All the time."

It is three-fifteen before we leave Osman's home with Kuchnicki, piled into Osman's truck with Kuchnicki's dog, Sunée, a shepherd-coyote mix salvaged from the pound. Arriving at the roadside at four, we take eight minutes and forty-five seconds—Osman times our progress—to hike up to the base of the ice.

Osman's new icefall is thin but ready to climb. There are three notable lines up the wall; each of them, if climbed on lead, will become a new route. Osman will lead the longest, to the left, with Kuchnicki belaying. He starts up at five o'clock, ascending thirty feet with delicate tool placements before placing his first screw. At the base of the icefall, ignoring Kuchnicki's warnings, Sunée lunges and snaps at chips of falling ice. It begins to snow. The ice is thin, and Osman climbs with even greater circumspection than he did on the Inertia Tube. By the time he tops out, sets a top-rope anchor, and lowers to the ground it is well after six. He tentatively rates the unnamed route a 5. Kuchnicki will climb next; I will belay.

Kuchnicki flicks on his headlamp and starts up the middle route on top rope at 6:55. It is pitch-dark, still snowing lightly. From the direction of the lake comes the mournful cry of a coyote. Climbing with confidence, Kuchnicki tops out in fifteen minutes and lowers off. Osman congratulates him. I follow, scaling the right side in good time, but get in trouble on the traverse. I flail for a minute without success and finally call for tension, lowering off the route several feet from the top.

As we break down our gear, Osman ponders names for his new route. Kuchnicki's climb—to say nothing of my own, aborted attempt—did not qualify as a first ascent thanks to the top rope. Kuchnicki plans to return within the week and lead the same line before another climber scoops the first, legitimate ascent. During the discussion of route names, Kuchnicki reveals to us that he intends to establish a rock climb entitled *Skippy's Revenge.*

. . .

Glittering in floodlights, a column of blue ice towers sixty feet above Osman's fenced backyard. Braced between two pines, a curtain of orange netting at its heart, the artificial ice climb is fed through a black, electrically heated hose attached to the house. Water drips steadily through a trickle device of Osman's design. Drawing from materials salvaged from the job site's dump, he constructed the climb over two afternoons in December. Sheltered from the day's sun by a tarp strung from the trees like a sail, growing in the consistently freezing temperatures at night, the column has taken more than two months to attain its present girth. Six or eight feet in diameter at its base, the gradually tapering icefall appears hinged; the upper third leans several degrees away from the house. Several weeks ago, the column cracked as Osman neared the anchor bar, lashed to the pines at its peak. With Osman still on his front-points, clinging to his tools, the upper third of the column shifted and dropped several feet, bending the steel support bars and settling at its present angle. Cemented in its new position with fresh ice, the upper section of the climb now offers a deceptively challenging overhang to a climber on the fall's north face. An attorney has told Osman that his homegrown ice climb could qualify as an "attractive nuisance" in legal parlance. Like an unfenced swimming pool, it may serve as a dangerous lure for neighboring children in the climber's absence.

After midnight, Osman is still climbing. With his truck backed up behind the house, Metallica plays unobtrusively from the open cab. The temperature is twenty-two degrees. Inside, Nikki and Coral are asleep. At Osman's invitation, we have been joined by sixteen-year-old Dustin Sabo, a promising young rock climber and freshman at Lake Tahoe Community College. With Kuchnicki belaying, Osman leads up the column's south face, placing a screw and an ice hook before topping out at the anchor bar and lowering off. Kuchnicki climbs next, this time on lead; he clips into Osman's two pieces as he ascends and places another screw between them.

Meanwhile, with Sabo belaying, I top-rope the north side and burn off on the overhang. Osman gives Sabo an introductory ice climbing lesson—a 5.12 rock climber, the youth has never worn crampons—and I belay him as he practices on the north side up to the overhang. Osman studies his progress closely, coaching. "It's not like rock climbing," he tells Sabo. "You want to stay over your crampons. Take shorter steps." Hanging from his tools, Sabo taps politely at the ice with his front-points. "Don't be tentative, Dustin," calls Osman. "Nail it. Make those placements count."

After lowering off the ice, Sabo takes a short rest and moves to the south side. In fifteen minutes he appears to have assimilated all of Osman's corrections, and front-points confidently up the south face, reaching the anchors without a fall. Belaying him, Osman is effusive with praise. Like Kuchnicki, Sabo appears to be a natural.

At one-thirty in the morning, Osman breaks to prepare a

bowl of microwaved popcorn for his guests. At Osman's request, Kuchnicki drives to the nearest gas station for a tray of instant hot chocolates.

The wooden front step to Osman's deck and front door is split in half. A fifteen-minute repair, the step has been broken for weeks. In this opportunistic era, the crevasse revealed by the split—broad enough to admit an unsuspecting foot and break an ankle—is a lawsuit in waiting. In the kitchen, sacks of garbage are piled like sandbags against the counter. Osman confesses that he has forgotten to put out the trash for three straight weeks. Eight months later the kitchen chair's foreleg is still broken. For one as concerned with form and precision as Osman the climber, his domestic carelessness is striking.

On the kitchen table a single red rose, dark with age, stands in a narrow glass vase. The water in the vase has long since evaporated. The drooping petals are dry and crinkly to the touch. Before the vase, in a basket, stands a wilting arrangement of mixed flowers. Elsewhere on the table lie a dirty bowl and spoon, a red hairband, a black watch cap, and a stack of children's books, including *A Horse and His Boy*, by C. S. Lewis, and *Hop on Pop—the Simplest Seuss for Youngest Use*. The empty hull of half an avocado lies on the kitchen counter. Gloves, jackets, pile sweaters, snowboarding boots, running shoes, scraps of paper, empty water bottles, and other debris lie scattered across the carpet and furniture in the main room. Five snowboards lean in the corners.

Osman's study is gradually beginning to resemble Jay Smith's gear room. In one corner, cams, ascenders, harnesses, pulleys, wall hammers, ice screws, étriers, ice axes, chains of carabiners, chalk bags, packs, and twelve coiled ropes in different hues hang from neatly spaced wall hooks. Spools of rope and cord of varying diameters stand on the floor, near boxes of expansion bolts, drill bits, plastic ice climbing boots, and a mound of loaded gear bags. A slender fishing rod leans in two parts on the windowsill. In context, given the industrial rigor of the climbing gear, the rod looks frail and quaint. I try to imagine Osman, sitting quietly on the end of a dock, fishing. The image is absurd and somehow unsettling. In my world, I realize, Osman is not allowed to sit on a pier and fish. No matter what I decide to do, I have doomed Osman, for the purposes of my mythology, to remain Osman. I am aware of his flaws, yet he remains for me essentially heroic. Not simply for his skill and courage but for his modesty, his essential graciousness. And yet like all heroes, living or dead, he is less himself, in my mind, than who I require him to be. And while I fear for his welfare, I know that if he were to stop jumping—or worse, to stop climbing—part of me would feel betrayed, as if by changing, Osman had disrupted the balance of the natural world.

A carpeted low balance beam stands in the middle of the living room. Leaning against the bricks of the fireplace is a framed poster, under glass, of Osman—a tiny, dancing figure sailing across a bottomless canyon on a six-hundred-foot Tyrolean traverse. Like the autographed print on Maliska's wall, it is a promotional poster for an outdoor clothing manufacturer; in bold letters the message reads: "The best view of one's soul is from beyond the edge, looking back."

The refrigerator door is quilted with photographs: there are shots of Coral, Nikki, and her sisters. There is a picture of Osman and Maliska, both shirtless, grinning under a sign that reads, "No Jumping from Bridge." There is a shot of Kuchnicki, Culp, and three other climbers gathered around the jumping anchor on the green steel walkway under the span. Two of them make a victorious, enthusiastic gesture—their thumbs and little fingers extended like horns from an upraised fist. Originally a surfer's sign for "hang ten," the sign, like the vocabulary of surfing itself, has gained widespread use among snowboarders, sport climbers, and others as a greeting and generic validation of all things bitchin' or rad.

Closest to the camera is Bob Aaron, a carpenter, climber, and extreme skier. In the photograph he is flushed, wide-eyed, crazed with elation. Months after this shot was taken, over breakfast in Meyers, he described his jump to me as the single most powerful experience of his life. "There's nothing like it," he said. "It's like stepping out to die."

There is a photograph of Nikki in the air, the tawny, tree-spotted valley far below. Her back is arched, her head flung back. Her feet are apart, her arms upraised and trailing. Her hands are open, fingers wide. I have seen video of this jump, and remember vividly her expression, composed but stricken with fear, as she balanced on the girder's edge. In the snapshot, taped to the refrigerator, there is a quality of surrender. Active surrender, not retreat. The snapshot is reminiscent of Robert Capa's celebrated photograph of the Spanish Loyalist, caught by the shutter at the instant he was struck and killed by a Fascist bullet near Cerro Muriano in 1936. He appears to have been running when he was hit. He is dead in the air, falling backward with his arms flung wide. He has not yet hit the ground. Even more, Nikki's posture in the photograph recalls the Louvre's *Winged Victory of Samothrace.* Carved circa 190 B.C.E., this eight-foot sculpture of the goddess Nike was unearthed centuries later in a farmer's field. The prize of the museum's classical collection, the sculpture stops you dead as you ascend the stairs. The figure is headless, without arms. But she retains her wings, and the deep folds of her gown stream as if in the wind. The goddess of victory is little more than a torso, a battered monolith of marble, but she soars.

As I stand in Osman's kitchen and consider the photographs, I realize with perfect certainty that I will not jump from the bridge. At the moment, this feels like a profound loss—not so much of the jump itself, but of what it signifies. With care, I will continue to climb. Over time, I may be at greater statistical risk in the mountains than I would be in a conclusive, isolated jump on Osman's rope. But the jump, in the end—and what it has to offer—isn't worth it. The decision is entirely my own. I suspect that I may never know a greater fear, or a greater benediction, than that which I knew in the hours surrounding my daughter's birth. If I do, it will not be on that bridge. Whatever befalls me, I doubt it will be in the mountains. If, indeed, I do again encounter such a fear, I suspect that it will again be at sea level, on dry land, in one of the many quiet rooms and corridors of ordinary life.

When I'm home, late at night, I often creep into the bedroom and approach my daughter's crib. I adjust her blanket, put socks on her feet without her waking, and gently cup her head with my hand. I tilt my head, bend down, and stare at her through the white wooden bars in disbelief. In these moments, despite her perfect health, I sometimes feel impelled to pray for her. I usually fight it, ashamed of the impulse. I'm being superstitious, I think. In any case, I decide, despite my experience in the hospital, I am not officially religious, and prayers are the property of churchgoers. I don't even know the words. Sometimes, in this way, the impulse gradually passes. At other times, despite these objections, I say a few stilted words under my breath.

Throughout a youth spent largely in pursuit of fear, I never for a moment suspected where I would find its source. We all draw lines, spontaneously or after long reflection, and every one that matters is a kind of death. And yet each line is an offering, less a bar of closure than a circle, inscribed to shelter something we love more.

Back in the yard, Osman sharpens the picks of his ice tools with a file against the gate of his truck. He steps into his crampons and fires up the column's north side. It is shortly before two in the morning. In two hours the temperature has dropped from twenty-two to eighteen degrees. The ice has grown dry and brittle, and as he climbs, chunks of the column break off and rain down, reflecting into the low wooden fence with hollow thuds. Soon, a dim yellow light appears in the neighbor's doorway. A matronly, silhouetted shape appears briefly, peering out. Osman is on the overhang, flashing up the ice in the lights.

On a side table in Osman's living room, a bronze medal with a red, white, and blue ribbon lies atop a copy of a book entitled *What Your Second Grader Needs to Know.* The helicopter still hovers above the couch, but Spider-Man is nowhere to be seen.

.
.
.
.
.
.
.
.
.

afterword

In the early darkness of November 23, 1998, Dan Osman was killed in a 1,200-foot fall from Yosemite National Park's Leaning Tower. Following a jump of some eleven hundred feet—a world record—the rope broke at a point nearly two hundred feet above his harness. He must have understood, for an instant, that the system failed. He was almost certainly killed upon impact. Osman was thirty-five.

Osman and a number of friends had erected the equipment weeks before, and spent several days jumping on the gear before Osman was detained by authorities for a suspended driver's license and related offenses. On the afternoon of his death, Osman and a friend returned to the site to remove the gear. The equipment had been exposed to the early winter elements— snow, rain, cold nights, and warm afternoons with dramatic temperature swings—for over a month. The nylon climbing ropes in the system were almost certainly damp to the core at the time of the accident, and rope manufacturers estimate as much as a 40 percent decrease in rope strength while wet. In all likelihood, the rope broke at a point that had previously been knotted. The nylon fibers in the area of such a knot, already strained by the first series of jumps, would have been further weakened by the expansion and contraction caused by variations of humidity and temperature. That Osman considered the equipment sound is both surprising and a testament to his extraordinary faith in its strength. He was sure of one thing, he wrote in a personal letter just days before the accident, and that was that the rope would never break if properly rigged. Speculation that his decision to jump on the gear was in some way suicidal is unfounded. There is strong indication that Osman was intending to slow down, at least temporarily, and spend more time with his daughter. He made comments to that effect, and had proposed marriage to Nikki Warren a week prior to the accident.

I last saw him outside a climbing gym in San Francisco, three months before the accident. He was heading off to Yosemite, his red truck loaded with gear, a grand scheme turning in his mind. He was in great spirits, bounding with energy, and looked younger than when I'd met him three and a half years before. He was just standing there, on the sidewalk, but there was something in the air around him, a kind of glimmer. I had first noticed it on his solo of Earn Your Wings. Others who knew him remarked it. His father suspected it to be an unusual concentration of ki, or life force. I can certainly do no better.

In the dilating flash of time through which he fell, untethered, I hope that he was not afraid. He had earned that, certainly, if nothing else. A final moment of composure—not of resignation but of readiness, of welcome—for the sword stroke he could not elude.

A trust fund has been established for Osman's daughter Emma, age twelve at this writing. While one of the world's finest climbers, he had no insurance or assets at the time of his death. Donations may be sent to:

The Emma Osman Trust Fund
c/o Andrea Osman-Brown
1760 Roper Court
Reno, NV 89506

Andrew Todhunter writes for numerous national magazines on subjects ranging from rock climbing to nautical archaeology, including an ongoing series of articles for *The Atlantic Monthly*. Born in Paris, raised in the United States, he worked as a laborer and spent six months in the ruins of Europe and Egypt before earning a degree in ancient history at the University of California at Berkeley. A diver, sailor, and amateur climber, Todhunter lives in the New York area with his wife and young daughter.

Made in the USA
Lexington, KY
05 March 2011